# Launching a Business

# Launching a Business

## The First 100 Days

Bruce Barringer

*Launching a Business: The First 100 Days*

First published in 2013 by
Business Expert Press, LLC
222 East 46th Street, New York, NY 10017
www.businessexpertpress.com

ISBN-13: 978-1-60649-397-7 (paperback)

ISBN-13: 978-1-60649-398-4 (e-book)

DOI 10.4128/9781606493984

Business Expert Press Entrepreneurship and Small Business Management collection

Collection ISSN: 1946-5653 (print)
Collection ISSN: 1946-5661 (electronic)

Cover design by Jonathan Pennell
Interior design by Exeter Premedia Services Private Ltd., Chennai, India

First edition: 2013

10 9 8 7 6 5 4 3 2 1

Printed in the United States of America.

# Abstract

This is a hands-on book that focuses on the tasks that a new business owner must complete in the first 100 days of launching a business. Think of it this way. Imagine you've conceived a business idea, written a business plan, raised seed capital, and are set to launch your business on October 1. Now, what would you actually do on October 1, October 2, October 3, and so forth? How would you set your priorities? How would you know which tasks are the most urgent? Although the answers to these questions vary depending on the business, there are a set of key activities that all businesses must accomplish to get their businesses off to a good (and legally proper) start. Examples include securing the proper business licenses and permits, setting up a bookkeeping system, negotiating a lease, buying insurance, entering into contracts with vendors, recruiting and hiring employees, making the first sale, and so on. Broader issues such as developing a business model and building a brand will be touched upon. But the primary focus of the book will be on the practical issues that a business owner needs to accomplish, and needs to accomplish correctly, to get a business off to a good start.

As a means of prioritizing and tracking the activities that must be completed at the onset of a business, the book will teach business owners how to set up a "First 100 Days Plan." A template (titled First 100 Days plan) will be included in the book.

# Keywords

entrepreneurship, small business, start-up, launch, new business, business plan, seed capital, marketing, financial management, intellectual property, hiring employees, human resources, sales, operations, business licenses, bookkeeping

# Contents

# Introduction

## How to Navigate the First 100 Days of a Business

This book provides a template for navigating the first 100 days of a new business. Its focus is on the nuts and bolts aspects of setting up and running a business, rather than the product or service you'll sell. Think of it this way. Imagine you've conceived a business idea, written a business plan, raised seed capital, and are set to launch your business on June 1. Now, what do you need to do to get ready for June 1? When June 1 comes, what should your priorities be? How do you know what tasks to focus on and in what order? While the answers to these questions vary depending on the business, there are a set of key activities that all businesses must accomplish to get their businesses off to a good (and legally proper) start. Examples include securing the proper business licenses and permits, setting up a bookkeeping system, negotiating a lease, buying insurance, entering into contracts with vendors, making the first sale, and so on. Broader issues such as developing a business model and building a brand will be touched upon. But the primary focus of this book will be on the nitty-gritty issues that a business owner needs to accomplish, and needs to accomplish correctly, to get a business off to a good start.

The book is organized around the activities that must take place in the first 100 days of a business. The 100 days are split into two parts: prelaunch (days 1–30) and postlaunch (days 31–100). As a means of organizing and tracking the activities that must be completed during this period, the book will teach you how to set up and execute a "First 100 Days Plan." A template (titled First 100 Days Plan) is included in the book.

Although completing a First 100 Days Plan may at first glance appear to be a tedious process, a properly prepared plan can save a business owner a tremendous amount of time, money, and heartache by providing a mechanism for determining and checking off the activities that must be completed during the early stages of a business. There are many businesses that, once started, represent viable ongoing businesses. The trick is to get them started. Most people aren't familiar with the steps necessary to start a business. If you fall into this category (like most people do) don't wing it. The First 100 Days Plan is a step-by-step, common-sense template for the nuts and bolts aspects of launching a business.

## Benefits of Completing a First 100 Days Plan

There are three primary benefits to completing and executing a First 100 Days Plan.

First, it creates a critical path for the nuts and bolts aspects of launching a business. The term "critical path" is used in managing projects, like building a house or developing a software product. It specifies what needs to be done and the order in which the activities need to take place. For example, when building a house the electrical wiring inside the walls needs to be in place before the drywall is put it. While this is an obvious example, in more complex projects it's important to work out these details ahead of time to avoid delays, uncertainty, and rework. It's the same with starting a business. For example, if you were planning to open a daycare business in Oklahoma City, OK, and drove to the city building to obtain a license to operate a business, before they issued the license they would ask for (a) your Federal Identification Number, (b) your State of Oklahoma business license, and (c) zoning approval to operate the business at the address you plan to open the business at. If you didn't have one or more of these items, they would ask you to come back when you were ready. While this might seem like a minor inconvenience, it saves time and money to do things in the proper order.

The second benefit of completing and executing a First 100 Days Plan is that it helps you avoid mistakes. Some mistakes may be minor—like inadvertently posting a photo you don't technically have rights to on your company Web site. But some mistakes may be major. For example, if you're opening a retail store, you should have general liability insurance in place before you open, just in case someone comes into your store and trips on the carpet or injures themself in some other way, and then sues you. Similarly, a background check on potential employees, which can be obtained in most locations for as little as $20, may help a new business avoid a problematic hire. These are precisely the types of nuts and bolts issues that are included in the First 100 Days Plan.

The third benefit associated with completing and executing a First 100 Days plan is that it helps a new business owner develop good habits. Examples include:

- Create a good filing system.
- Add the copyright bug (©) to all original documents.
- Bill all completed work immediately.
- Date everything.
- Capture every customer's e-mail address.
- Making sure the proper signatures are being used in signing leases and contracts.

While individually these items may seem like little things, collectively they're the types of activities that help a business run smoothly. For example, in regard to creating a good filing system, many businesses use different color files to distinguish what's inside them: red for client files, blue for invoices, yellow for bills, green for projects, white for personnel, and tan for news clippings and articles. There is no better time to start developing good habits than during the initial rollout of a business. A section in the prelaunch phase of the First 100 Days Plan recommends that a filing system be established, and different color file folders be used to store different types of information.

## How to Complete the First 100 Days Plan for Your Business

The First 100 Days Plan for your business should be completed with your business clearly in mind. It's a tool that's meant to point you in the right direction rather than tell you exactly what to do. For example, state, city, and county governments differ regarding the requirements for licensing a business. As a result, the First 100 Days plan for a business started in Oklahoma City may vary from the plan for a similar business launched in Wichita. The type of business also makes a difference. People in certain professions, such as barbers, chiropractors, nurses, and real estate agents, must normally pass a state exam and maintain a special license to conduct business. Some businesses (such as interstate trucking) require a federal license to operate. There are also seemingly little things that catch business owners off guard if they're not paying close attention. For example, sign ordinances vary significantly from location to location. In some locations virtually anything goes, while in other locations signs can't be put up at all. In many jurisdictions, there are limits on how large signs can be.

The overarching point is each section included in the First 100 Days Plan covers as many contingencies as possible, but it isn't all-inclusive. You should remain on guard for additional start-up requirements that pertain to your specific business or are unique to your particular geographic location.

There are also judgment calls that you'll have to make. Some portions of the First 100 Days Plan alert you to things you should be thinking about, but it's your call whether to implement them. For example, will you accept credit cards? Will you offer your customers credit? If you offer your customers credit, how long will they have to pay? If they don't pay on time, what will you do about it? The First 100 Days Plan will alert you that you need to make these types of decisions, but the decisions are yours.

It's important to also recognize that your business won't be built in 100 days. It's just a start. It takes time to build a brand, establish a reputation, earn repeat business, hire good people, and so on. Still, the first 100 days are critical. It's during this period that you make your first impression, establish good (or bad) habits, avoid (or incur) costly mistakes, and win your first customers. If things go smoothly, it's a confidence builder. One of the keys to starting and running a successful business is believing that you can do it.

## Things You Won't Find in This Book

The things you won't find in this book are how to recognize a business opportunity, how to write a business plan, how to build a product, how to raise money, and how to determine if starting a business is the right choice for you. It's assumed that you have worked through these issues and are ready to go. As mentioned, The First 100 Days Plan focuses on the nitty-gritty. It helps ensure that you're not missing something major. The stakes are high. For example, if you start a business that sells a product, and neglect to collect sales tax, there are meaningful adverse consequences involved.

## The Plan for This Book

The book is divided into two sections as shown below:

Introduction
Section 1: Prelaunch (Days 1–30)
Section 2: Postlaunch (Days 31–100)

### Introduction

As discussed earlier, there are three primary reasons for preparing a First 100 Days Plan: Creating a critical path for the nuts and bolts aspects of starting a business, avoiding costly mistakes, and developing good habits. It also helps you stay organized and establish priorities. Starting a business is not an easy task. As a result, many business owners, when they're shown the First 100 Days template, say "I wish I had had something like this when I started my business." While the First 100 Days Plan is not meant to be a definitive checklist, it is a useful guide. It alerts you to the issues you should be thinking about during the initial rollout of your business.

### Prelaunch (Chapters 1–7)

These chapters deal with activities that should be completed before a business launches. In reality, for most start-ups, there is no clear "launch" date. The founder or founders gear up and at some point make a sale and the business is launched. While in most cases this works out alright, it's not ideal, and may expose the founder or founders to unnecessary risk. For example, if a business starts making sales before it addresses how it should be legally organized, it is a de facto sole proprietorship or general partnership, and the owners are subject to personal liability for the actions of the business. This risk can be removed by organizing as a subchapter-S corporation or a limited liability company (LLC), which is a simple thing to do, but it requires the filing of specific paperwork and it requires the business to comply with the rules of operating as a subchapter-S corporation or an LLC. Similarly, before a business can accept a check made out in the name of the business (rather than the name of the founder), it must obtain a fictitious business name permit and obtain the requisite city, state, and federal licenses to conduct business.

## Postlaunch (Chapters 8–13)

These chapters deal with activities that typically take place after a business launches. No business is completely ready to go the day it launches, so there is a natural period when the business is gearing up and putting all the pieces in place. Again, the focus of the First 100 Days Plan is on the nuts and bolts aspects of launching a business, which in the postlaunch phase include activities such as setting up a sales process, developing an operations plan, managing a business's money, and hiring employees. These are initiatives that will invariably be improved upon repeatedly throughout the life of a business. The objective of the First 100 Days Plan is to help the business get off to a good start in each of the areas, and to avoid pitfalls and mistakes.

In the last chapter of the postlaunch segment (Chapter 13), an important segment is included on the day-to-day challenges of operating a business. Business owners are sometimes surprised by how often they are distracted or interrupted at work, by the need to juggle multiple roles, by how time consuming it is to stay on top of government regulation and compliance issues, the pressures to succeed financially, and how challenging it is to achieve work–life balance. Fortunately, there are steps that business owners can take to cope with each of these issues in a sensible and healthy manner, and get the first 100 days of their business off to a good start.

# SECTION 1

# Prelaunch Days 1–30

# CHAPTER 1

# Legal Requirements Part 1

## Introduction

Each chapter begins with a list of the topics covered in the chapter, then proceeds to cover each topic. At the end of the chapter, the portion of the First 100 Days Plan just covered is displayed. Instructions are provided on how to complete each step in the First 100 Days Plan for that chapter.

| | |
|---|---|
| Step 1 | Select a Business Name |
| Step 2 | Select an Attorney or Reliable Alternative |
| Step 3 | Choose a Form of Business Ownership |
| Step 4 | Obtain a Federal Employer Identification Number |
| Step 5 | Obtain a Fictitious Business Name Permit |
| Step 6 | Register for Federal Licenses and Permits |
| Step 7 | Register for States License and Permits |
| Step 8 | Register for Local Licenses and Permits |
| Appendix | First 100 Days Plan: Legal Requirements Part 1 |

## Step 1: Select a Business Name

While, at first glance, naming a business may appear a minor issue, it is an extremely important one. A company's name is one of the first things people associate with a business, and it's the phrase they'll type into their computer, Smartphone, or GPS if they want to find you. A company's name is also the most critical aspect of its branding strategy. The name of a business must facilitate rather than hinder how the business wants to differentiate itself in the marketplace and how it wants to be viewed by customers.

There are several rules of thumb for how to select a name. If a company plans to focus on a particular type of customer, its name should reflect the attributes of its clientele. For example, a chain of clothing store that specializes in large sizes for men is called Casual Male XL. If a company plans to focus on a particular product or service, its name should reflect the advantages that its products or service brings to the marketplace. Examples include Anytime Fitness, Bark Busters, and Quality Fresh Seafood. There are also more general rules. Select a name that's easy to spell, easy to pronounce, doesn't mean something awkward or offensive in a foreign language (particularly Spanish), and doesn't limit the future expansion of the business. For example, a name like Kate's Smartphone Supplies isn't a good choice. It's easy to spell and pronounce, but at some time the business might want to expand beyond Smartphone supplies. You can try a made-up name if you'd like, like Google or Zynga. Sometimes this strategy works, but it takes more effort to help people associate your name with the clients you serve or the products or services you sell. You'll also have to obtain an Internet domain name. Most companies want their domain name to be the same as their company name. This can be tricky, because the most obvious domain names are already taken. Chapter 7 "Establishing an Online Presence" covers the topic on how to go about selecting a domain name.

There are steps that must be taken to make sure that the name you select hasn't already been taken and is available for use. The steps are shown in Table 1.1. It's extremely important that you follow these steps. If a business selects a name and later finds out that it has already been legally taken, the business may have to (1) amend its article of incorporation, (2) change its Internet domain name, (3) obtain new listings in telephone and other directories, (4) redo signage, advertising copy, stationary, business cards, and (5) incur the expenses and potential embarrassment of introducing a new name to its customers. You also cannot select a name that is slightly different but confusingly similar to a name that's already been taken. For example, if you opened a casual dining restaurant and name it Pandora Bread, both Pandora (the online music radio station) and Panera Bread (the casual dining restaurant) would undoubtedly argue that your name is confusingly similar to their name, and your ability to use Pandora Bread may be disallowed.

**Table 1.1. *How to Find Out if a Name for a Business Is Already Taken***

| Instructions | |
|---|---|
| 1. | Go to the United States Patent and Trademark (USPTO) Web site at uspto. gov. Click on the link labeled "Trademark Search." Enter the name you've chosen for your business. If the name has already been taken, you'll have to pick another name. |
| 2. | Visit the Secretary of State's Web site for the state in which you would like to register your business. Find the area dedicated to business services. Find a search box labeled something like "Business Entities Search" or "Business Name Search." Type in the name of your business. If the name has already been taken, you'll have to select another name. |
| 3. | In some states, there isn't a statewide search engine for business names. If this is the case in your state, check with your municipal government's office (if you live in a city or town) or your county clerk's office (if you live in an unincorporated area) to make sure your business name hasn't been already taken. |
| 4. | To see if the name you've picked has been registered by an Internet-based company, perform a search on one of the domain registration sites, like GoDaddy.com or Register.com. In some cases the name may have been registered, but not for the purposes of operating a business. If it's clearly a business, you may have to pick another name. |

## Step 2: Select an Attorney or a Reliable Alternative

If most cases, you'll want to select an attorney to help you choose a form of business ownership and assist you with other legal issues. If you do this, pick an attorney who is familiar with start-up requirements and has successfully led other business owners through the start-up process. It's often not necessary to pay an attorney his or her advertised rate. Many attorneys recognize that start-ups are short on cash and will either reduce their rates or work out an installment plan or other payment arrangements to get the business the legal help it needs. This is particularly true if the attorney senses that the new venture has strong commercial potential and may develop into a steady client in the future. The best way to find an attorney is ask other business owners in your area who they would recommend.

While hiring an attorney is advisable, it is not the only alternative available for researching and filing the necessary forms to get a business up and running legally. Most business owners can do much of the legwork on their own, and rely on an attorney for guidance and advice. If you're extremely tight on money or feel like you can handle the legal process on your own (which is not generally recommended but may apply in some cases), there are Web-based companies that can help you with the necessary forms and filings. Examples include LegalZoom (www.legalzoom.com), Rocket Lawyer (www.rocketlawyer.com), and Nolo (www.nolo.com). All three Web-based companies provide a comprehensive menu of legal services for business owners, including the ability to ask lawyers questions for modest fees. It's a judgment call on your part whether to hire an attorney to do your legal work; utilize a service like LegalZoom, Rocket Lawyer, or Nolo; or pursue a blended approach. A blended approach might involve hiring an attorney to obtain legal advice (such as determining your form of business ownership) and then utilize one of the Web-based services to prepare the documents and file them with the appropriate governmental agencies on your behalf.

## Step 3: Choose a Form of Business Ownership

Before a business is launched, a form of legal entity must be chosen. It must be chosen early, because the subsequent steps, such as obtaining a Federal Employee Identification Number and securing certain licenses and permits, require you to identify your form of legal entity. There are four forms of business ownership to choose from: sole proprietorship, partnerships, corporations, and limited liability companies (LLCs). Ideally, you'd be fully up to speed on the subtleties of each form of business ownership before you have made your decision, but that's rarely the case. Most business owners rely on the advice of their attorney or accountant, or make the decision themselves. For those who make the decision themselves, online legal document preparation services such as those mentioned above can help and the IRS provides a tutorial on each form of business ownership at www.irs.gov. There are also seminars conducted through various organizations that help new business owners get up to speed. For example, the Oklahoma Tax Commission provides free workshops for prospective business owners to acquaint them with the legal aspects of starting a business in Oklahoma. Advice can also be obtained via nonprofit organizations, such as SCORE (www.score.org), that assist business owners.

There is no single form of business ownership that works best in all situations. Most businesses launch as either subchapter-S corporations or limited liability companies. The following is a brief synopsis of each form of business ownership.

### Sole Proprietorship

The simplest form of business ownership is the sole proprietorship. It involves one person, and the business and the person are essentially the same. Sole proprietors report their income and expenses on Schedule C of their individual tax returns. The biggest advantage of the sole proprietorship is that the owner maintains complete control over the business. The biggest disadvantage is that the sole proprietor is responsible for all the actions and liabilities of the business. If a sole proprietor's business is sued, the owner could theoretically lose all the business assets along with personal assets. As a result, a sole proprietorship is not a good choice for most business owners.

Advantages of a sole proprietorship:
- Creating one is easy and inexpensive.
- The owner maintains complete control of the business and the profits.
- It is not subject to double taxation (explained later).
- The business is easy to dissolve.

Disadvantages of a sole proprietorship:
- Liability on the owner's part is unlimited.
- The business ends at the owner's death or loss of interest in the business.
- Raising capital can be difficult.
- The liquidity of the owner's investment is low.

### Partnerships

If two or more people start a business, it must be organized as a partnership, corporation, or LLC. Partnerships do not pay taxes—rather the income or loss incurred by the partnership is passed through to the partners' individual tax returns. Partnerships are organized as either general or limited partnerships. The primary advantage of general partnerships is that the business is not dependent on a single person for its success. The primary disadvantage is that the individual partners are liable for all of the partnership's obligations. As a result, a general partnership is not a good choice for most new businesses.

Advantages of a General Partnership:
- Creating one is easy and inexpensive.
- The skills and abilities of more than one individual are available for the business.
- It is not subject to double taxation (which is explained later).

Disadvantage of a General Partnership:
- Liability on the part of each of the partner is unlimited.
- Disagreements among partners can occur.
- The liquidity of each partner's investment is low.

The second form of partnership is the limited partnership. The primary difference between the two is that a limited partnership includes two classes of owners: general partners and limited partners. The general partners are liable for the obligations of the partnership, but the limited partners are liable only up to the amount of their investment.

### Corporations

A corporation is a separate legal entity organized under the authority of a state. Corporations are organized as either C or subchapter S corporations. A C corporation is a legal entity that is separate from its owners. The major advantage of a C corporation is that it shields its owners from personal liability for obligations of the business. The major disadvantage is that a C corporation is subject to double taxation—the corporation is taxed on its net income and, when the same income is distributed to shareholders in the form of dividends, it is taxed again on the shareholder's personal income tax returns. Very few businesses organize as C corporations initially.

Advantages of a C Corporation:
- Owners are liable only for the obligations of the corporation up to the amount of their investment.
- No restrictions on the number of shareholders.
- The ability to share stock with employees through incentive plans can be a powerful form of employee motivation.

Disadvantages of a C Corporation:

- Setting up and maintaining one is more time consuming and more expensive than a sole proprietorship or general partnership.
- Business losses cannot be deducted against the shareholder's other sources of income.
- Income is subject to double taxation.

A subchapter S corporation combines the advantages of a partnership and a C corporation. It is similar to a partnership in that the profits and losses of the business are not subject to double taxation. Instead, the corporation's taxes are passed through to its shareholders' individual tax returns. It is similar to a C corporation in that the owners are not subject to personal liability for the obligations of the business. The major disadvantage of the subchapter S corporation is that it is limited to 100 shareholders, which can be a drawback when trying to raise money from a large pool of investors. A large percentage of start-ups organize initially as subchapter S corporations.

### Limited Liability Company

The limited liability company (LLC) is a form of business ownership that is gaining popularity. The main advantages of the LLC are that it is more flexible than is a subchapter S corporation in terms of number of owners and tax-related issues, and all members enjoy limited liability. Similar to a subchapter S corporation, an LLC does not pay taxes. Instead, the corporation's taxes are passed through to its shareholders' individual tax returns. The main disadvantage of a subchapter S corporation is that it is more time consuming and expensive to set up than a sole proprietorship or a general partnership, and in some states the rules governing the LLC vary. A large percentage of start-ups are organized initially as LLCs. The owners of an LLC are called members rather than shareholders.

Advantages of an LLC:

- Members are liable for the obligations of the business only up to the amount of their investment.
- The number of shareholders is unlimited.
- There is no double taxation.

Disadvantage of an LLC:

- Setting up and maintaining one is more time consuming and expensive than the other legal entities.
- Some of the regulations governing LLCs vary by state.
- Some states levy a franchise tax on LLCs, which is essentially a fee the LLC pays the state for the benefits of limited liability.

### Special Note for Professionals

If you are a professional, such as a doctor, a dentist, a lawyer, an engineer, or an accountant, you should seek out special advice from an attorney or accountant before starting a business to practice your profession. Certain professionals are able to form corporations referred to as "professional corporations" or "professional service corporations." Typically, a professional corporation is organized for the sole purpose of providing professional services. For example, in a dental corporation, all the shareholders must be licensed dentists.

Dentist, doctors, and other professionals start professional corporations to obtain favorable tax treatment (which has become less generous over time) and to place limits on personal liability. Generally, if a group of doctors incorporate as a professional corporation, and a specific doctor in the corporation is sued for malpractice, the other doctors would be shielded from liability if the doctor who was sued was held liable.

## Step 4: Obtain a Federal Employee Identification Number

You need a Federal Employee Identification Number (normally called an Employer Identification Number or EIN). The only exception is if you plan to be a sole proprietor and will have no employees. You obtain an FEIN number by filling out and submitting IRS form SS-4. The easiest and quickest way to do this is to go to www.irs.gov and then click on Apply for an EIN Online. The process is straightforward. You can also download and complete form SS-4 in longhand, and then call the IRS at 1-800-829-4933 to register by phone. If you'd prefer to file for your

FEIN by mail, you can obtain Form SS-4 at www.irs.gov and mail it to the address shown on the form.

## Step 5: Obtain a Fictitious Business Name Permit

If you plan to use a fictitious name, which is any name other than your name, you'll need to obtain a fictitious business name permit (also called *dba* or *doing business as*) in most instances. If the business is a sole proprietorship, the permit can usually be obtained at the city or county level. If the business is a partnership, corporation, or limited liability company, the permit is normally obtained via the state's Secretary of State's office. The way this works is that if your name is Melanie Ryan and you apply for a business license, your business will be registered as Melanie Ryan. If you want to use another name, like Mountain Fresh Fish, you'll need a fictitious business name permit. This requirement generally applies regardless of the form of business ownership you choose.

## Step 6: Register for a Federal Licenses and Permits

Most businesses do not require a federal license or permit. However, several types of businesses do. Table 1.2 contains a partial list of the business activities that require a federal license or permit, along with the Web site address of the federal agency to contact. If you visit the Web site of one of the federal agencies shown in Table 1.2, and are still unsure about how to proceed, the best thing to do is to contact your state's Secretary of State's office, and ask for help. In most cases, they'll be able to direct you to the specific division within the federal agency to contact. The #1 rule is if you're uncertain, ask. Severe penalties can be levied if you sell an item or provide a service that requires a federal license or permit and you do not have the required license or permit.

As with all licenses and permits, another approach for learning what you need is to ask someone who is currently operating a business very similar to the one you plan to start. Most prospective business owners are surprised to find that existing business owners are generally more than willing to answer questions and help new business owners in other ways.

*Table 1.2. Partial List of Businesses That Require a Federal License or Permit to Operate*

| Business activity | Web site address of federal agency to contact |
|---|---|
| Alcohol or Tobacco sales (including microbreweries and small wineries) | www.aft.gov |
| Aviation | www.faa.gov |
| Drug manufacturing | www.fda.gov |
| Firearms, ammunition, and explosives sales | www.aft.gov |
| Ground transportation | www.dot.gov |
| Income tax preparation | www.irs.gov |
| Investment advising | www.sec.gov |
| Preparation of meat products | www.fda.gov |
| Radio or television broadcasting | www.fcc.gov |
| Wildlife-related activities | www.fws.gov |

# Step 7: Register for State License and Permits

In most states, there are four different categories of licenses and permits that you may need at the state level.

## Professional Licenses or Permits

In all states, there are laws that require people in certain professions to pass a state examination and maintain a professional license to conduct business. Examples include barbers, chiropractors, nurses, tattoo artists, land surveyors, psychologists, social workers, and real estate agents. Requirements vary from state to state, so the best thing to do is check with your state's Secretary of State's office.

## Occupational Licenses and Permits

There are also certain businesses that require a state occupational license or permit to operate. Examples include plumbers, daycare centers, trucking companies, and insurance agencies. Similar to professional licenses and permits, requirements vary from state to state, so the best thing to do is check with your state's Secretary of State's office.

### Sales Tax Permit

Most states and communities require businesses that sell goods and, in some instances, services to collect sales tax and send them to the proper state and local government authorities. Sales tax rules vary from state to state, and city to city, so you'll need to check with your state's Secretary of State's office and your local municipal and county governments. Normally, if you're obligated to collect sales tax, you must get a license from your state. Once you start making sales, you'll then be required to calculate the applicable sales tax, collect it from the customer, keep tax records, and then file a tax return and pay the taxes in your state. Depending on your level of sales, you'll pay taxes monthly, quarterly, or annually.

If you plan to make sales to out-of-state buyers or clients, check with an accountant or your local tax authorities. Rules get complicated for collecting sales tax for out-of-state sales.

### Business Registration Requirements

Some states require all new businesses to register with the state, even if they do not require a professional or occupational license or permit. For example, the state of Oklahoma requires new businesses to complete a several-page document titled "Oklahoma Business Registration Application" prior to commencing business. The purpose of the document is to (1) register the business, (2) place the business on the radar screen of the tax authorities, and (3) make sure the business is aware of and complies with certain regulations, such as the need to withhold state and federal taxes from the paychecks of employees. Again, the best way to determine if your state has a similar document is to contact your state's Secretary of State's Office or conduct an online search. Many states support a Web site that provides a step-by-step guide on how to start a business in their state. For example, the Vermont Secretary of State's Office has a link on its Web site titled "A Checklist for Starting a Business in Vermont" (www.sec .state.vt.us/corps/start.htm). The 26-item checklist includes items that all new businesses in Vermont must comply with, along with items that are relevant to only certain businesses. For example, all retail businesses that sell products must collect sales tax, but only businesses that plan to put up a sign need to comply with sign ordinances. Some regulations are very specific. For example, in Vermont, no outdoor advertising is permitted other than on-premise signs with a total area of not more than 150 square feet. If you weren't aware of the sign ordinance, and have put up a sign of 200 square feet, you would have to take it down.

## Step 8: Register for Local Licenses and Permits

### Local Licenses

On the local level, there may be licenses and permits that you have to obtain. If you live in a city or town, you'd get them at your local municipal building. If you are in an area outside a city or town, you go to the county courthouse. Cities and towns vary in terms of the licenses and permits you need and the order in which you need to get them. For example, Table 1.3 depicts the local requirements for opening a business in Atlanta, GA.

*Table 1.3. Local Requirements for Opening a Business in Atlanta, GA*

| 1. | Go to the Zoning Enforcement Division, located at 55 Trinity Avenue SW, Suite 3900, Atlanta, GA 30303, to verify that your business is located within the city limits of Atlanta, and obtain approval for your business location. |
|----|----|
| 2. | Fill out the New Business Tax Application Form available online at www.atlantaga.gov/government/finance/businesslicense.aspx. To fill out the New Business Tax Application Form for your business you'll need to know—your business's name, start date, location, Federal Employee Identification Number, State Tax I.D. Number, and number of employees. You will also need to have information about the owners of the business such as their names, addresses, and social security numbers. |
| 3. | Take your zoning approval, your completed New Business Tax Application Form, a photo ID, proof that your business is incorporated (if applicable), and a $75 nonrefundable registration fee to the City of Atlanta Business Tax Division, 55 Trinity Avenue, SW, Suite 1350, Atlanta, GA, 30355. Checks are not accepted. |

### Local Permits

There are two categories of local permits that may be needed.

The first is a permit to operate a certain type of business. In Atlanta, for example, there are many businesses that need additional permits (or licenses). Examples are vendors that sell goods in private establishments or on public property, adult or child care services, businesses that sell alcoholic beverages, hotels and motels, and businesses that involve massage salons or technicians. Many cities also have quirky requirements, which vary from city to city. For example, in Atlanta, you need a permit to operate a business that involves billiard or pool rooms.

The second category is permits for engaging in certain types of activities. Examples are as follows:

- Building permit: Typically required if you are constructing or modifying your place of business.
- Health permit: Normally required if you are involved in the preparation or sale of food.
- Occupational permit: May be required if you are opening a home-based business.
- Signage permit: May be required to erect a sign.
- Alarm permit: Sometimes required if you have installed a burglar or fire alarm.
- Zoning permit: Generally required if you are developing land for specific commercial use.
- Fire permit: May be required if a business sells or stores highly flammable material or handles hazardous substances.

### Important Final Notes

The Small Business Administration supports a Web site that provides a useful starting point for determining the types of business licenses and permits that are needed in specific areas. The site is available at www.sba.gov /content/business-licenses-and-permits. You simply type in your zip code and select from a menu of business types, and the site generates a list of the types of licenses and permits that you'll likely need to obtain in your area.

There are also fee-based online services that will research the business licenses and permits you need. An example is Business Licenses at www.businesslicenses.com. For either $99 or $199, depending on how comprehensive a service you want, the service will research the federal, state, county, and local licensing requirements for your business and provide you with a full Business License Compliance Report. This type of service can be very helpful if you can afford the fee.

# APPENDIX
# First 100 Days Plan

**Prelaunch (Days 1–30)**

*Part 1: Legal Requirements Part 1*

|  | Requirement | Check when done | Result (fill in below) |
|---|---|---|---|
| Step 1 | Select a Business Name | ☐ | Select a name for your business and explain the rationale for the name |
| Step 2 | Select an Attorney or a Viable Alternative | ☐ | Describe how you would approach this issue. Your choices are select an attorney, utilize a reliable alternative, or pursue a blended approach. If you opt to utilize a reliable alternative, identify who or what the alternative would be. If you choose the blended approach, provide a description of your specific approach. |
| Step 3 | Choose a Form of Business Ownership | ☐ | Select a form of business ownership and explain your rationale. |
| Step 4 | Obtain a Federal Employer Identification Number | ☐ | Describe how you would obtain an FEIN. |
| Step 5 | Obtain a Fictitious Business Name Permit | ☐ | Determine if your business needs a fictitious name permit. If it does, explain how you will get it. |

| | Requirement | Check when done | Result (fill in below) |
|---|---|---|---|
| Step 6 | Register for Federal Licenses and Permits | ☐ | Determine if your business requires any federal licenses or permits. If it does, identify the licenses and permits that you'll need, how you'll go about getting them, and what they'll cost. |
| Step 7 | Register for State Licenses and Permits | ☐ | Determine if your business requires any state licenses or permits, and if it needs to register at the state level. If it does, identify the licenses and permits that you'll need, how you'll go about getting them, and what they'll cost. Also, identify any state registration requirements that apply. |
| Step 8 | Register for Local Licenses and Permits | ☐ | Determine if your business requires any local licenses or permits. If it does, identify the licenses and permits that you'll need, how you'll go about getting them, and what they'll cost. |

# CHAPTER 2

# Legal Requirements Part 2

## Introduction

This chapter contains an overview of additional legal issues that may or may not apply to your start-up. It's important to review each issue. While some of the issues, such as negotiating a lease, may not apply to you initially, they may apply at some point in the future. If an item is relevant it's important that you address it now. An investment of a small amount of time and money now can result in an exponentially larger amount of saved time and money down the road.

Note—this section is not all inclusive. There are legal issues pertaining to topics such as hiring, taxes, and intellectual property covered in other sections of the First 100 Days Plan. There may also be legal issues not covered in this book that are unique to your business.

| Step 1 | Drafting a Founder's Agreement (if applicable) |
| Step 2 | Preparing a Buyback Agreement (if applicable) |
| Step 3 | Negotiating a Favorable Lease |
| Step 4 | Executing Fair and Valid Contracts |
| Step 5 | Nondisclosure Agreement |
| Step 6 | Writing a Code of Business Conduct |
| Appendix | First 100 Days Plan: Legal Requirements Part 2 |

## Step 1: Drafting a Founder's Agreement

If you are starting a business with one person or more, it's important to have a founders' agreement. A founders' (or shareholders') agreement is a written document that deals with issues such as the relative split of the equity among the founders of the firm, how individual founders will be compensated for the cash or "sweat" equity they put into the firm, and how long will the founders have to remain with the firm for their shares to fully vest.

The items typically included in a founder's agreement are shown in Table 2.1.

*Table 2.1. Items Included in a Founders' (or Shareholders')*
*Agreement*

- Nature of the prospective business.
- Identity and proposed titles of the founders.
- Legal form of business ownership.
- Apportionment of stock (or division of ownership).
- Consideration paid for stock or ownership share of each of the founders (may be cash, real property, or "sweat equity").
- Identification of intellectual property signed over to the business by any of the founders.
- Description of how the founders will be compensated and how the profits of the business will be divided.
- Basic description of how the business will be operated and who will be responsible for what.
- Description of the outside business activities that the founders will not be allowed to engage in (e.g., you wouldn't want a founder to engage in an outside business that directly competes with your business).
- Provisions for resolving disputes (many founders' agreements include a stipulation that disputes will be resolved via mediation or arbitration rather than through the courts).
- Buyback clause, which explains how a founder's shares will be disposed of if he or she dies, wants to sell, or is forced to sell by legal order.

## Step 2: Preparing a Buyback Agreement

A buyback agreement (or buyout agreement) is a binding contract among the founders of a business that controls the buying and selling of ownership interests in the business. It's usually included in the founder's or shareholders' agreement. It addresses what happens to the equity of a founder if the founder:

- Decides to leave the business
- Want to sell to an outsider
- Seeks to buy out a cofounders' interest in the business
- Becomes physically or mentally disabled
- Dies

The agreement generally includes a buyback (or buyout) clause, which legally obligates the departing founder to sell to the remaining founders his or her interest in the business if the remaining founders are interested. In most cases, the agreement also specifies the formula for computing the dollar value to be paid. The presence of a buyback clause is important for at least two reasons. First, if a founder leaves the firm, the remaining founders may need the shares to offer to a replacement person. Second, if a founder leaves because he or she is disgruntled, the buyback clause provides the remaining founders a mechanism to keep the shares of the firm in the hands of people who are fully committed to a positive future for the business.

## Step 3: Negotiating a Favorable Lease

Almost all new businesses start out either in their founder's home or in a leased space. In fact, many businesses, even as they grow, prefer to remain in a leased space, to avoid tying up capital in real estate and to remain flexible if the space requirements of their business changes. (Note: A subsequent section of the First 100 Days Plan focuses on finding the right location for your business).

A lease is a contract between you and a landlord. It can be for a short term (less than a year) or for an extended period (several years). There are two primary considerations in negotiating a lease: (a) setting the tone for the negotiations and (b) the content of the lease. It's important that you take the process of negotiating a lease seriously. For many new businesses, the lease they sign is their largest financial obligation.

### Setting the Tone for the Negotiations

There are four things to be mindful of as you prepare to negotiate a lease. First, when you first engage a landlord, you'll be presented with a typed lease. It will totally favor the landlord so consider it a starting point. If you're an attractive potential tenant, chances are you'll be able to negotiate more favorable terms. Second, keep in mind that you have dual goals. You want to negotiate a favorable lease, but you also want to have a good long-term relationship with your landlord. Third, a good negotiating strategy is to ask for equal treatment. For example, if the landlord requires you to fix something you're responsible for within 10 days, then the land-lord should also be required to fix something he or she is responsible for within 10 days. Finally, remember your ultimate objective is to secure space that works for your business at an affordable price. Getting the best combination of quality space and affordable price involves trade-offs. For example, if you're cash-strapped and you're interested in a property that will require major renovations before you can move in, it may be more important to you to ask the landlord to pay for 50% of the renovations than to try to negotiate a lower monthly rent.

You should do your homework before commencing negotiations. You should know the going rate for rental property in the area you're interested in, and have a good idea of how large of a space you'll need. You should also recognize that there are trade-offs between negotiating a short-term lease versus a long-term lease. A short-term lease means less commitment for you, but will work against you in incentivizing your landlord to pay for improvements to modify the property to suite your needs. Don't be penny wise and pound foolish in securing property. You may have to pay the going rate or even a premium to secure the ideal loca-tion for your business.

It's important to know that many landlords are less likely to budge on monthly rent than any other demand, particularly if the property is a multiunit building. That's because they want to tell prospective tenant D that tenants A, B, and C are all paying $20 or more per square for their space (or whatever their rent is). Tenants A, B, and C may have negotiated other concessions, but landlords like to standardize rent. They do this to maintain consistencies in their cash flows and just in case tenant D isn't a savvy negotiator.

### The Content of the Lease

There are a number of common items that are included in leases. Table 2.2 lists 13 important items, and how should you approach each of the items as the potential lessee. If one or more of these items isn't in the lease, and they're relevant to your business, you should do your best to get them included.

*Table 2.2. Thirteen Common Items in Leases and How You Should Approach Them*

| | Common items (issues) in leases | How you should approach them |
|---|---|---|
| 1. | Who should sign the lease? | If your business is a corporation or a limited liability company (LLC), then the lease should be in the name of the business, and you should sign as president or CEO of the business. The landlord may want you to personally guarantee the lease. It's a judgment call whether do this—sometimes it's required to secure the property you want. If you guarantee the lease, you'll be responsible for the payments if the business can't make them. |
| 2. | Define the Space You're Leasing | Make sure the lease specifically defines the space you're renting, and gives you rights to use common areas, such as the parking lot, entryway, and hallways. If the landlord agrees to pay for a service, like having a dumpster emptied once a week, make sure that benefit is spelled out in the lease. If you're paying on a square foot basis, you should measure the square footage yourself to make sure you're getting what you pay for. |
| 3. | Start Date of the Lease | Make sure the start date is clearly specified, and that there is a provision in the lease that specifies what happens if the space you're renting isn't ready the day you plan to move in. This is particularly important if you're leasing space in a building that's under construction, because construction delays are common. Make sure you're not obligated to pay rent until you can occupy your space. |
| 4. | End Date of the Lease | Make sure the lease has an end date. Normally, a lease will state if the tenant stays in the property beyond the end date and has not exercised an option to renew the tenancy if from month to month at the discretion of the landlord during the holdover period. |
| 5. | An Option to Renew the Lease | While you'll probably want a short-term lease (1–2 years), the landlord may try to pressure you to sign a long-term lease (2–4 years). The ideal compromise may be a 2-year lease with an option to renew for an additional 2 years. Be prepared to pay a higher initial monthly rent if you negotiate an option to renew at the same monthly rate. This is because an option to renew at the same rent is an arrangement that is typically more favorable for the tenant than the landlord. |

*(Continued)*

*Table 2.2. Thirteen Common Items in Leases and How You Should Approach Them (Continued)*

| | Common items (issues) in leases | How you should approach them |
|---|---|---|
| 6. | Rent | Leases usually state the rent on a monthly basis. There is typically a penalty if the rent is paid late. If the lease is for more than a year, it will often include an escalation clause, meaning that the rent can go up in future years. There is typically a formula in the lease that stipulates how rent in future years is determined. Make sure the formula makes sense. A common method is to tie to the Consumer Price Index. You should resist a formula that bases your future rent on increases in your landlord's operating expenses. There should also be a cap on how much your rent can increase in a single year. |
| 7. | Improvements to the Property | If the space you'll occupy needs improvements before you move in (like new carpet), make sure the lease specifies the improvements the landlord has agreed to make. If the landlord has authorized you to make improvements, make sure the lease specifies the improvements that you have permission to make. The lease should also specify when the improvements the landlord has agreed to do will be done. Insist that the improvements be done before you move in. |
| 8. | Restrictions on Use of Space | Make sure any restrictions on the use of the space you're renting aren't too restrictive. For example, if you're renting space to open a book store, make sure the lease doesn't restrict you to only selling magazines and books. At some point you might want to open a coffee bar for your patrons, so you'll want your lease to provide you that flexibility. |
| 9. | Right to Expand | If you're renting space in a building that has other tenants, or vacant space, try to negotiate the right to add adjacent space when it becomes available, or to move to larger quarters in the same building. Sometimes this is done through a right of first refusal. A right of first refusal means that the landlord must make vacated space available to you first, before renting it to another business. |

*Table 2.2.  (Continued)*

| | Common items (issues) in leases | How you should approach them |
|---|---|---|
| 10. | Subletting Your Space or Assignment the Lease | These are tough things to negotiate, but if you can try to negotiate the right to sublet your space or even assign your lease to a third party; for example, rather than setting up your own coffee bar, you might sublet space in your bookstore to a local coffee shop to set up the coffee bar. Similarly, if you need to move out of your space before the lease expires, try to secure the right to assign your lease to a third party. If your landlord won't go for an assignment clause, try to negotiate a dollar amount to pay to terminate the lease. You want an escape clause if your business fails or you need to move for some other reason. |
| 11. | Termination Clause | You should try to negotiate an option to terminate your lease early. You want an escape clause if your business fails or you need to vacate for some other reason. Your landlord will normally insist on a fixed dollar amount to terminate the lease or an amount equivalent to a certain number of months' rent, like three months. This is normal and is a concession you may need to make to get a termination clause in the lease. |
| 12. | Mediation or Arbitration | Try to have a clause included that requires mediation or arbitration if there is a dispute between you and the landlord. Mediation and arbitration are faster and cheaper than lawsuits. |
| 13. | Signs | If you plan to erect a sign, make sure the lease gives you the right to do so. |

There are additional areas in which you should conduct due diligence. You should make sure the premise complies with the Americans with Disabilities Act (ADA) and that the area in which the property is rented is properly zoned for your business. Don't take a landlord's word for it that the area in which the property is located is zoned for your type of business. Check with local authorities before you sign the lease.

## Step 4: Executing Fair and Valid Contracts

As a business owner, you'll enter into contracts with landlords, lenders, suppliers, service providers, customers, and others. A contract is a written agreement between two or more parties that is enforceable by law. Most contracts are simple legal documents. They set out mutual promises to perform some type of act. For example, Business A promises to pay Business B $2,000 if Business B builds it a Web site and completes it on or before May 1.

For most contracts, there are standard forms available that can be obtained through an Internet search or through a service like Nola (www.nola.com), which sells templates for most types of contracts online. Nola also sells inexpensive books ($20 to $30 range) which contain CD-ROMs with templates for business contracts and other startup documents.

All contracts must contain the following four elements, to be considered valid:

- All parties are in agreement.
- Something of value has to be exchanged. A contract doesn't have to involve money. It can be barter for goods or services. For example, in the illustration shown previously, assume Business A is a consulting company. Business A could have promised to provide Business B 10 hours of consulting services in exchange for building its Web site instead of $2,000. Of course, Business B would have to agree to this arrangement.
- In a few situations, such as the sale of real estate, the agreement must be in writing. Of course, because oral contracts are hard to enforce, it's best to get all contracts in writing.
- The contract must be signed by the relevant parties.

There are two levels of information you need to know about contracts as a new business owners: contract basics and how to negotiate a favorable contract.

## Contract Basics

There are several elements that you should be particularly attentive to when either preparing or reviewing a contract. These are outlined in Table 2.3.

*Table 2.3.* **Contract Basics**

| | Basic elements of contracts | Explanation |
|---|---|---|
| 1. | Names | Be sure that the names of the parties to the contract and the signatures are in the correct format. If the contract is between two subchapter-S corporations, the contract should be in the corporate names of each party. If the contract involves a sole proprietorship that is operating under a fictitious name, the name of the owner and the fictitious name of the businesses should be on the contact. For example, if Jack Petersen (sole proprietor) is operating his business as CleanTech Services (fictitious name), he should sign contracts as Jack Petersen, doing business as CleanTech Services. |
| 2. | Signatures | The same goes for signatures. If your business is a corporation or an LLC, you should designate your form of business ownership and the state in which you're incorporated after your name when signing a contract. For example, if you're a C-corporation named Madison Networks, you were incorporated in Wisconsin, and the CEO's name is Brad Kramer, the signature line should read Madison Networks Inc., A Wisconsin Corporation, By Brad Kramer, CEO, 110 Badger Ave., Madison, Wisconsin, 53705. |
| 3. | Personal Guarantees | If you're the founder of a new or a young firm, you'll often be asked to personally guarantee the contract, even if you're organized as a corporation or an LLC. It's a judgment call whether to do this. If the contract is important to you (like a loan to fund your business) and the party on the other side of the contact won't budge, you may need to agree to the personal guarantee to get the contract signed. Just know that you're now on the hook for the entire amount of the contract if your business can't pay. Sometimes your spouse will also be asked to sign. |
| 4. | Customized or Limited Guarantees | Sometimes you can negotiate a customized or limited guarantee. For example, you may place a clause in the contract that states "I personally guarantee the terms of the promissory note. However, the maximum amount of my liability is $25,000." Instead of guaranteeing a dollar amount, you might guarantee a restricted time. For example, you might negotiate a clause that states, "I personally guarantee the terms of the promissory note for a period of 36 months from the date of the note." |

*(Continued)*

*Table 2.3. Contract Basics (Continued)*

| | Basic elements of contracts | Explanation |
|---|---|---|
| 5. | Contract Templates | There are many standard templates for contracts. Most are designed to be equally fair to both parties, so they're generally ok to use. Any point, however, in the standard contract can be negotiated and changed, as long as both parties agree. Don't be intimidated by a written contract that's nicely formatted and looks like nothing can be changed. It can. |
| 6. | Attachments | Many contracts contain attachments, which spell out terms that the parties have negotiated that are not part of the standard contract. For example, you may sign a standard lease agreement with a landlord, but negotiate that the landlord hires a snow removal service to clear the parking lot of your building when it snows. Rather than trying to figure how to incorporate this provision into the standard lease agreement, you can include it in an attachment to the contract. |
| 7. | Amendments | Once a contract has been executed, it can be changed only if all the parties involved agree and sign an amendment. For example, a business may be experience financial stress and tell its landlord it simply can't afford the rent it's paying. The landlord (to keep the tenant) may agree to reduce the rent. Don't rely on a verbal agreement. An amendment to the contract should be prepared that specifies the new rent. It should be signed by all parties. |
| 8. | Resolving Disputes | The contact should specify how the parties involved will resolve disputes. Typically, mediation or arbitration is quicker and less expensive than utilizing the courts. |
| 9. | Copies and Storage | In most cases, an original copy of the contract should be provided to each of the parties involved. An exception is a promissory note, in which there is only one original note, which is kept by the lender until the note is paid off. You should store the original copies of your contracts in a safe place, like a fireproof container or a bank safe deposit box. If your originals are stored in some place other than your office, make sure you have copies to quickly refer to. |

## How to Negotiate a Favorable Contract

There are many books, articles, and Web sites that provide advice on how to negotiate a favorable contract. While the advice and tips provided by these resources can be helpful, most experts argue that the best contract is one that's fair to all parties involved. In fact, if you're ever in a situation where someone has made a mistake or they're confused and offer you a contract that's extremely in your favor, pause before signing it and weigh the risks. While the contract may be legally enforceable, you may ruin or damage a relationship, because eventually the other party will figure out what happened and may resent the fact that you didn't alert them to an obvious misunderstanding or mistake.

Still, there are techniques that help business owners negotiate the best terms possible. The most commonly mentioned techniques are as follows:

- Start early. Don't wait until a week before you need space to start looking. The reason negotiating contracts is featured in Chapter 2 of this book is to give you time. You shouldn't rush into signing major contracts. If you are rushed, try not to signal that to the party you're negotiating with. If they're savvy negotiators, they'll use your need to get something done quickly to their advantage.
- Do your homework. Make sure that you know what the going rate is for the item or items you're negotiating. For example, if you hire a Web design firm to design your Web site, you should find out what the common rate is for the type of Web site you're wanting. Ask around. If the common rate is $2,000 and the firm you're negotiating with wants $4,000, you can tell them that you've done the research and their stated rate is too high.
- Don't give in too hastily. It's natural that when you're trying to get a business up and running to try to get agreements consummated quickly. Resist this temptation when negotiating contracts, particularly if there is significant money at stake. If the Web design firm referenced earlier won't budge on their price, tell them to justify their price or look elsewhere. Make sure they know they might lose the deal if they don't lower their fee.

- Get professional support. If you're negotiating a high dollar contract, like a long-term lease for office or commercial space, it may be money well spent to hire an attorney to negotiate the deal for you. Make sure to get an attorney who is familiar with negotiating leases. Remember, if you only negotiate contracts occasionally, and the party you're negotiating with does it frequently, you're at a competitive disadvantage. In this instance, the only way to level the playing field is to hire an attorney who does it frequently too. While it may sting to pay an attorney $1,000 or more to negotiate a contract, that amount may be recovered quickly if the attorney can negotiate more favorable terms than you could on your own.
- Be wary of someone who won't negotiate reasonable requests. If you're asking for a small concession, and the other party won't even consider it, that's a red flag. It's an indicator how reasonable the other party will be for the duration of the contract. Some deals aren't worth making.

## Step 5: Nondisclosure Agreement

A nondisclosure agreement is a written agreement that binds an employee or other party (such as a consultant or a vendor) to not disclose a company's trade secrets. Even if you don't have trade secrets now, you will once your business is launched. Technically, a trade secret is any formula, pattern, physical device, idea, process, or other information that provides the owner of the information with a competitive advantage in the marketplace. Trade secrets include customer lists, marketing plans, product formulas, financial forecasts, employee rosters, logs of sales calls, and laboratory notebooks. More information about trade secrets is provided in Chapter 5, Protecting Your Intellectual Property.

Once you start hiring employees, it's a good idea to have each of your employees sign a nondisclosure agreement. The Federal Economic Espionage Act passed in 1996 criminalizes the theft of trade secrets, so a nondisclosure agreement has teeth to it. The idea is to prevent a current

Nondisclosure Agreement. This nondisclosure agreement is effective as of _____ (the effective date) by and between _____ (the employee) and _____ (the business). The agreement has no expiration date.

At all times _____ (the employee) agrees to refrain from disclosing _____ (business's name)'s customer lists, trade secrets, and/or other confidential material.
_____ (employee's name) agrees to take reasonable security measures to prevent accidental disclosure and industrial espionage.

IN WITNESS WHEREOF, _____ (employee name) and _____ (company name) have signed this agreement.

_____ (employee signature)

_____ (officer of business signing on behalf of the business)

_____ Date

*Figure 2.1. Sample nondisclosure agreement.*

or former employee, or a third party that's privy to your trade secrets, from sharing them with others. Figure 2.1 provides an example of a nondisclosure agreement you might want to ask your employees to sign. This is a straightforward agreement. Templates for more detailed nondisclosure agreements are available online. FindLaw (www.findlaw.com) provides an excellent discussion on how to effectively draft and use nondisclosure agreements.

## Step 6: Writing a Code of Business Conduct

Most new businesses get into legal trouble as a result of misunderstandings, sloppiness, or a simple lack of knowledge of the law. Getting into legal trouble is something that a new business owner should work hard to avoid. Not only is it time consuming to work through legal disputes, but it can also damage the reputation and status of a new firm.

A document that can help a business to avoid legal disputes is a Code of Business Conduct. A Code of Business Conduct is a formal statement of an organization's values on certain ethical and social issues. The advantage of having a Code of Business Conduct is that it provides specific guidance to the employees of a business regarding expectations of them in terms of ethical behavior.

There are three primary steps that new businesses can take to avoid legal trouble. These steps, which are described next, should be an integral part of every business's Code of Business Conduct:

### Meet All Contractual Obligations

It's important to meet all contractual obligations on time. This includes paying people and businesses as agreed and delivering goods and services as promised. If an obligation can't be met on time, the problem should be communicated to the affected party as soon as possible. Nothing is more irritating to suppliers, for example, when not only are they not paid on time, but the company that owes them money doesn't even extend them the courtesy of calling to make arrangements to catch up. If enough time passes and there is no communication between the affected parties, it could trigger a lawsuit.

### Get Everything in Writing

Many business disputes arise because of the lack of a written agreement. Although it is tempting to try to show business partners that you trust them by not insisting on a written contract, this approach is usually a mistake. Disputes are much easier to avoid if the rights and obligations of the parties involved are in writing. For example, what if the business referred to earlier that hired the Web design firm for $2,000 to design its Web site didn't insist on a written contract, and the Web design firm promised to deliver a "good looking Web site" "as soon as possible." The two parties could easily later disagree over the quality and functionality of the finished Web site and the project's completion date.

### Operate Fully Within the Law—Even in Little Things

Finally, it's important to operate fully within the law. While this recommendation may seem obvious, it's not always the case. Sometimes business owners simply don't think and this can lead to legal trouble. For example, say you're designing your Web site and you capture images from other Web sites to use on your site. Legally, you can't do this, unless you have written permission to use the images you're capturing or you know they're in the public domain. You might think to yourself, "No one will ever notice or care." That's not the right mentality for a business owner. You should operate within the law. There are Web sites that provide access to free images and companies that sell images, like Getty Images (www.gettyimages.com). Even then, you have to follow the rules. For example, FreeDigitalPhotos.net is a site that provides access to free images and sells images. If you use a free image, you must publish an acknowledgment to FreeDigitalPhotos.net on the same page or screen where the image is used. A similar example is if you buy a single seat or license to use a software product, you shouldn't look for a way to let three of your employees use it. If you need three licenses, buy three licenses. When you purchase the license from the software vendor, you'll be asked to sign an agreement that stipules that it's a single license. Never sign a contract or an agreement and knowingly operate outside the intent of the contract or agreement.

A Code of Business Conduct can also include other ethics-related issues, such as avoiding conflicts of interest, and issues that are specific to a particular business. For example, if you are starting a business that will serve food, you may want to include a section in your Code of Business Conduct that deals with personal hygiene and how that relates to the preparation and servicing of food.

Table 2.4 provides an example of a Code of Business Conduct. You should develop a Code of Business Conduct even if you're starting your business as a sole business owner. You should sign and date the agreement, and require future employees to sign and date the agreement as part of their terms of employment. If you use this sample as a starting point for your own Code of Conduct, substitute your business's name for Company A in the document.

*Table 2.4. Sample Code of Business Conduct*

| Company A |
|---|
| 1. | Compliance with Laws, Rules, and Regulations<br>All employees and officers of the company are required to respect and obey the laws, rules, and regulations of the cities, states, and countries in which we operate. |
| 2. | Meeting Contractual Obligations<br>All employees and officers of Company A are required to meet and enforce the contractual obligations that the company has entered into. If a contractual obligation (such as a loan payment or a payment for supplies that is due by a certain date) cannot be met, it is the responsibility of the employee overseeing that account to contact the relevant party immediately (i.e., within three business days) to make arrangements to meet the obligation. If an employee is not sure if he or she is responsible for the account or is not sure how to proceed, the employee should seek advice from a supervisor or other appropriate personnel. |
| 3. | Getting Agreements in Writing<br>All employees and officers of the company are required to place agreements with outside stakeholders in writing. Outside stakeholders include lenders, landlords, suppliers, business partners, and customers (to the extent reasonable). |
| 4. | Conflicts of Interest<br>A conflict of interest exists when an employee or officer's private interest interferes in any way, or even appears to interfere, with the interests of Company A.<br>A conflict situation can arise when an employee or officer takes actions or has interests that may make it difficult to perform his or her company work objectively, effectively, and professionally. Conflicts of interest may also arise when an employee or officer, or a member of his or her family, receives inappropriate personal benefits as a result of his or her position in the company. It is a conflict of interest if a company employee or officer also works for a competitor, customer, or supplier. Employees should avoid any direct or indirect business connection with customers, suppliers, or competitors; except those required through normal duties on behalf of the Company A.<br>Conflicts of interest are prohibited as a matter of company policy, expect as approved by the board of directors. If you have a question about what constitutes a conflict of interest, you should consult with your supervisor. |
| 5. | Competition and Fair Dealing<br>We seek to outperform our competition fairly, honestly, and honorably. Employees pledge to seek competitive advantage on behalf of Company A through superior performance and never through illegal or unethical business practices. Each employee and officer should endeavor to respect the rights of and deal fairly with Company A's customers, suppliers, competitors, employees, and external stakeholders. |
| 6. | Annual Acknowledgment<br>To help ensure compliance with this Code of Business Conduct, the company requires that all employees and officers review the Code of Business Conduct and acknowledge their understanding and adherence in writing at the time of initial employment and thereafter on an annual basis on the attached form. |

Your Personal Commitment to
Company A
Code of Business Conduct

I acknowledge that I have receive a copy of Company A's Code of Business Conduct dated _____, that I have read the Code and that I understand it, and that I will comply with it. If I learn that there has been a violation of the code, I will contact my supervisor immediately to disclose what I know.

Dated: _____


_____

Employee's Signature


_____

Employee's Name (Please Print)

# APPENDIX

# First 100 Days Plan

## Prelaunch (Days 1–30)
### Part 2: Legal Requirements Part 2

| | Requirement | Check when done | Result (fill in below) |
|---|---|---|---|
| Step 1 | Drafting a Founder's Agreement | ☐ | Assume you're starting your business with another person, in the manner you selected in the previous assignment (in terms of form of business ownership). Draft a simulated Founders Agreement for your business. |
| Step 2 | Preparing a Buyout Agreement | ☐ | Note: This step can be skipped if a buyback agreement is part of your Founder's Agreement. Assume you're starting your business with one other person, in the manner you selected in the previous assignment (in terms of form of business ownership). Prepare a simulated Buyout Agreement for your business. |
| Step 3 | Negotiating a Favorable Lease | ☐ | Assume you're leasing property to locate your business. Describe the type of property you'll be looking for (square foot, location, any special requirements). Identify the going rate for a similar property in the area in which you want to locate. Make a list of the things that would be important to you in negotiating a lease. |

*(Continued)*

## Part 2: Legal Requirements Part 2 (Continued)

| | Requirement | Check when done | Result (fill in below) |
|---|---|---|---|
| Step 4 | Executing Fair and Valid Contracts | ☐ | Think of the types of contracts that your business will enter into. Select one contract (whether it is with a vendor, customer, distributor, or someone else). Describe what would the contract consist, what would be the key points, and make a list of the things that would be important to you in negotiating the contract. |
| Step 5 | Nondisclosure Agreement | ☐ | Assume you'll be hiring employees. Prepare a simulated Nondisclosure Agreement for your business. |
| Step 6 | Writing a Code of Business Conduct | ☐ | Write a simulated code of business conduct for your business. |

# CHAPTER 3

# Getting Up and Running

## Introduction

This chapter focuses on the tasks required to get a business up and running. Each of the tasks can be done casually and quickly, or seriously and deliberately. It's important that you choose the latter. Choosing a poor location (particularly for a retail store), obtaining inadequate insurance, or failing to put business systems in place can stymie the success of a new business. The same holds true for setting up an office and establishing a filing system. A well-designed office and an efficient filing system can contribute to the smooth functioning of a business as much as any other activity.

These are also activities that should be done or at least started at the prelaunch stage. For example, once you launch your business, you'll be too busy to be thinking about the design of your office. It is best if that step has been completed or is well underway before your business launches.

| Step 1 | Choosing a Location |
| Step 2 | Obtaining Insurance |
| Step 3 | Setting Up an Office |
| Step 4 | Establishing a Filing System |
| Step 5 | Create Business Systems (From the Beginning) |
| Appendix | First 100 Days Plan: Getting Up and Running |

## Step 1: Choosing a Location

An important issue for any business is its location. A good choice of location can help a business get off to a good start, while a poor choice can have the opposite effect. A poor choice can also be difficult to fix, particularly if a business purchases a property or signs a long-term lease.

For some businesses, location is critical, while for others it's a nonissue. For example, many service businesses—such as carpet cleaning services, painters, electricians, and Internet companies—don't interface directly with the public, so their physical location isn't a major issue. In fact, these businesses often seek out nondescript locations to economize on costs. In contrast, location is an extremely critical issue for retail stores, certain service businesses (like a quick printing service), or professional practices (like a dentist's office) that deal directly with the public.

The rest of the information on choosing a location is organized in three topics: rules of thumb for businesses where location is important, how much you can afford, and determining whether the physical structure you're considering is adequate for your business.

### Rules of Thumb for Businesses Where Location Is Important

The key consideration here is to pick a location that will increase your volume of customers. Start by asking yourself the following questions:

- Will my customers come on foot or public transit, or will they drive and need a place to park?
- Will more customers come if the business is located near other similar businesses?
- Will more customers come if the business is located near complementary businesses?
- Do the demographics of the trade area in which the business will be located make a difference?

Answering these four questions can go a long way in helping a business owner select an appropriate location. For example, if you're opening an urban bagel shop, you'll want to locate in an area that has a high amount of foot traffic. In contrast, if you're opening a fast-food restaurant or a convenience store, you'll want to be on a busy street where the business can be seen by drivers who can pull into your parking lot. Sometimes the side of the street you locate on is critical. For example, if you're opening a donut shop (donuts are a morning food) on the edge of town, you'll want to be on the side of the street where drivers on their morning commute into town can pull into your business without having to cross traffic.

In terms of being near to similar businesses, jewelry stores and clothing stores, for example, often benefit by being near similar businesses, since people like to comparison shop. A hair salon, where comparison shopping isn't as much of an issue, may do better on its own. Some businesses benefit by locating near a Wal-Mart or Target, because their customer bases are similar and they benefit from the increased traffic. Similarly, some businesses benefit by being located near complementary businesses. For example, a day spa may benefit by being located near a nail salon that doesn't offer any massage or facial treatments.

An extremely important issue is whether the demographic makeup of a trade area is suitable for a particular business. A high-end furniture store, for example, needs to be in an affluent area. Stores that sell children's clothing do better in areas with a high percentage of young families than in areas with a high percentage of retirement-age people.

### How Much Can You Afford?

This is a tough issue, because the best locations are invariably the most expensive. As mentioned in Chapter 2, Legal Requirements Part 2, most new businesses that aren't home-based lease property rather than build or buy, which reduces the cost for some. The best way to determine the rental rate for a particular area is to talk to a real estate agent or property management company. Ultimately, a business can only occupy premises it can afford. There is no formula for making this determination—it's a judgment call. In some cases, a business such as an urban bagel shop may be better off spending a disproportionate amount of its money on a premium location, and cut back in other areas, such as marketing or the restaurant's décor.

### Is the Physical Structure You're Considering Adequate?

Once you locate a property to lease or rent, you should be careful to make sure that it's adequate for your business. For example, if you will be cooking in a building, the smoke and steam from the stoves may need to be vented in a certain manner, requiring additional plumbing and electrical work to be done. Similarly, if you'll be operating an Internet-based business, certain additional wiring may be necessary. It's often a matter of negotiation regarding who will pay for these upgrades, as noted in Chapter 2. There are other issues that are potentially negotiable, so make sure you think through your situation carefully. For example, if you open a retail store in an enclosed mall or a strip mall, you can often negotiate what's called a restrictive covenant to prevent the landlord from leasing space to one of your direct competitors.

Complying with local zoning laws is another principal issue. Don't take a landlord's word that a property is zoned for a particular purpose. Check with the zoning authorities yourself. Never put a penny into a building (leased or owned) until you're absolutely sure that it's zoned for the business you intend to operate.

## Step 2: Obtaining Insurance

There are two sources for business insurance: working through a local insurance agent or obtaining insurance from an online site that will help you shop for the best rates. Both approaches work. For new business owners, it may be preferable to work with a local agent, who can perform a comprehensive audit of the insurance you need and coordinate coverage. To find an agent, ask other business owners in your industry for a referral. If you're opening a restaurant, for example, it would be to your advantage to work with an agent who is familiar with the insurance needs of restaurants. Don't be afraid to interview several insurance agents before you select the one you're most comfortable with. Also, in most cases, it's better to have an insurance agent who can obtain quotes from several companies, rather than being tied to a single provider.

When you're talking to your insurance agent, be inquisitive. For each policy, make sure you know what's covered and what's not. For example, if you own the building you occupy and buy property insurance, are damages from an earthquake covered? How about water damage from leaking or burst pipes? What if a falling tree damages your roof in a storm? Is the roof covered? How about the $2,000 it costs to remove the tree? Some of these risks can be covered by paying a small extra premium, but you might have to ask to find out.

There are five types of insurance you should be thinking about in preparing to open a business: property insurance, business interruption insurance, liability insurance, workers' compensation insurance, and health insurance.

### Property Insurance

If you're leasing property, you'll need what's called a standard commercial renter insurance policy (sometimes called small business property insurance). It protects the equipment, machinery, inventory, and furnishings in a business space leased or rented from someone else. Your landlord's property insurance doesn't cover these items. The standard commercial renter policy covers your personal property against fire, smoke, theft, vandalism, and the water damage not caused by a flood. Most standard policies do not cover damage caused by a flood or earthquake. You have to buy supplemental flood and earthquake insurance to protect against these hazards.

If you are leasing, make sure you read the insurance portion of your lease before you buy any property insurance. You may have agreed to insure the building as if you were the owner (try to not let this happen when you're negotiating a lease). If you did, you'll have to buy the appropriate insurance. If you or one of your employees causes physical damage to your landlord's property as a result of negligence, you may be liable. Even if your landlord's property insurance covers the loss, the insurance company may come after you to recover its payment.

If you own the building you're operating your business from, make sure you buy coverage for the premises and the business personal property inside the premises (i.e., equipment, machinery, inventory, and furnishings). It's usually best to insure your premises and business personal property for 100% of its replacement value. Some policies only cover the current value of the property rather than the replacement value. You want a policy that covers the replacement value.

Nearly all insurance includes a deductible. So whatever your damages are, you'll get a check for the damages less the deductible. Larger deductibles result in lower premiums. Be careful not to buy a policy with a deductible that's so large that it would be a financial hardship on your business to pay the deductible.

### Business Interruption Insurance

Business interruption insurance covers the loss of income that your business would suffer if the facilities it occupied were damaged or destroyed until the business could be rebuilt (or you relocated). A property insurance policy only covers physical damages; it does not compensate you for loss of income. Normally, business interruption insurance is not sold on a stand-alone basis. Instead, it is something that you bundle with your property insurance coverage.

### Liability Insurance

There are different types of liability insurance.

Most businesses buy a general liability policy. This policy covers your business if someone is injured on your property or if you cause damage to the property of others. In certain situations, a general liability policy also protects the property of others. General liability policies typically state a dollar limit per occurrence and a total limit for the policy year. For example, your policy might state that it will pay up to $250,000 per occurrence for personal injury not to exceed $1 million in any one policy year. It's extremely important to have general liability insurance. If you don't, a single claim could wipe out your business.

For businesses that sell products, product liability insurance is available. This policy provides coverage for injuries caused by products you design, manufacture, or sell. Product liability coverage is expensive, so it's typically bought by businesses that sell products that could potentially injure someone, like chemicals. If you're a retailer who sells potentially hazardous chemical in its original package, your exposure is greatly reduced. The most likely litigant in a lawsuit would be the manufacturer. You're also provided a certain level of coverage in your standard commercial renter policy. If your business applies in any of these situations, you should check with your insurance agent.

If your business will own vehicles or your employees will use their vehicles for business-related purposes, you'll need special liability coverage. The coverage for your employees' vehicles is called Employer's Non-Owned Automobile Liability Insurance and is relatively inexpensive. Of course, if your business will own cars, delivery vans, or trucks you'll need standard vehicle insurance on them.

### Workers' Compensation Insurance

Workers' Compensation Insurance is a special type of liability insurance that covers your liability for injuries that employees suffer on the job. All businesses with three or more employees are required to provide for some kind of workers' compensation coverage. Rules pertaining to workers' compensation insurance vary by state. Most small businesses buy workers' compensation insurance through a private insurance carrier, which may be a for-profit or not-for-profit provider. Some states have state funds. For an individual business, workers' compensation rates are based on the industry and occupation, the size of the business' payroll, and in some cases the company's safety record. Workers' compensation insurance is required only for employees, and not for independent contractors. Sole proprietors do not have to buy workers' compensation insurance for themselves.

The way workers' compensation insurance works is that if an employee is injured on the job, he or she is entitled to wage replacement and medical benefits in exchange for agreeing to not sue the employer for negligence. Damages for pain and suffering are usually not available through workers' compensation plans. Some states have panels or commissions that oversee the proper administration of workers' compensation in their state.

### Health Insurance

There are two levels of consideration for health insurance—how you insure yourself as the business owner and whether you'll provide health insurance to your employees.

In regard to the business owner (or owners), you'll need to obtain insurance through a private insurer if you're not making arrangement for a group policy for you and your employees. Health insurance is a major expense. In most areas, it costs $12,000 a year or more to purchase family coverage. If you're leaving a job where you were provided health insurance, one option is to keep that coverage and pay the premium in full. This option is available through the Consolidated Omnibus Budget Reconciliation Act, or COBRA. COBRA allows people who leave jobs to remain covered by the employer's group policy for up to 18 months, with the employee paying the entire premium (plus a 2% administration fee). If the business you're leaving had less than 20 employees, COBRA doesn't apply.

Ultimately, you'll have to weigh whether buying private insurance or going the COBRA route (if it's available to you) is the best option. A big advantage of COBRA is that it provides you continuous coverage—you don't have to change doctors or prove insurability. It's tough to be without health insurance, particularly if you have a family, so the cost of health insurance is often a major issue for people in deciding whether to leave a job and start a business.

If you're not able to obtain health insurance through traditional means, as a result of the cost or a preexisting medical condition, don't give up before you do some digging. There are a growing number of private and public programs to help expand access to health insurance.

You'll also need to decide whether you will provide health insurance to your employees. For employers who provide benefits, these generally include health insurance (sometimes including dental and vision benefits), term life insurance, and possible disability insurance. Some employers also provide a retirement plan. In terms of health insurance, employers can provide coverage for employees and may also include their families. Most employers pay for a portion of the insurance, and ask employees to pay for the balance. Most small businesses that offer health insurance aren't large enough to make it economical to act as the sole policyholder for their employees' insurance. Instead, they pool their employees with other business's employees to form a multiple-employer trust. The trust is then the policyholder. This strategy allows small businesses to benefit from the lower premiums and other services enjoyed by larger groups. Sometimes businesses can organize the health insurance they provide their employees through a trade or professional organization.

# Step 3: Setting Up an Office

It's important to think carefully about how you'll set up your office. Depending on your circumstances, you may also have to design, furnish, and equip offices for employees, shared workspaces, a reception area, and a meeting room. What should not be done is to throw together an office and other workspaces on the fly. You and your employees need workspaces that are organized, efficient, pleasant to work in, and equipped with the technology necessary to service your customers in an effective manner.

There are four major considerations in setting up an office: office design, furnishing an office, office equipment and supplies, and communications equipment and software. Setting up an effective filing system will be covered in Step 4 of this chapter.

## Office Design

The way you design your office, and the workspaces in your business, is important. Map out an efficient work flow. Make sure that the equipment you use most frequently will be within easy reach. If possible, plan flexibility into the space with a desk that won't be impossible to move, moveable equipment and adjustable shelving. As your business grows, your work flow may change and you want the flexibility to rearrange your office accordingly.

Make sure to apply common sense in the design, and consider how furniture and systems work together. For example, your shredder should be located near a trash container so it will be easy to empty. Similarly, your printer paper should be stored near your printer for efficient replenishing. Good lighting is critical. Arrange lights so you can turn them on and off in various work areas as the need arises. Place noisy equipment away from areas where you need silence. For example, it's not a good idea to place your printer next to your phone. If you want to print while you're on the phone, the noise from the printer will be a distraction. Plan where you'll put the equipment that needs electricity with the location of the electrical outlets in mind.

Your office should also be pleasant. Although it's a workspace, it should be a place where you enjoy spending time. Ergonomics, the study of the spatial design of job requirements and work sites in relation to human physical and psychological capabilities and limitations, has become an important component of designing workspaces. You should decorate your office but not to a fault. If it's important to you to have a large whiteboard on the wall where you can brainstorm, scribble notes, or record your schedule for the coming week, the whiteboard should have priority over a painting.

If you're starting a business where you need to create a certain atmosphere, you should keep that in mind. For example, if you're a financial planner, your office should project financial success. If you're opening a counseling service, you'll need an office that's substantial enough where people feel comfortable talking without fear of being overheard outside.

A good way to see how offices are laid out is to visit an office furniture store and ask for a catalog. Manufacturers of office equipment print catalogs that show dozens if not hundreds of different office layouts using their furniture. Office furniture salespeople will also help you plan your office, and even visit your premises to measure your space and make recommendations. These folks are particularly helpful if you're designing a suite of offices, a reception area, or a break room, where the choices are less familiar and the design is more complex.

### Furnishing an Office

You need adequate but not necessarily expensive furniture. You can often economize by watching for auctions or sales. There are also used office furniture stores in many cities. If you would want to buy new, stores like Wal-Mart and Office Depot have a fairly wide selection of cheaper desks and filing cabinets. It's a careful balance. You want to economize, but also want to create an office that has the qualities described in the previous section.

An L-shaped desk works best for most people. It gives you a place for your computer and printer, plus desk space that is completely open. You should have a comfortable swivel chair for yourself and at least two stationary chairs facing your desk. The number of file cabinets and bookshelves you'll need varies by business. Make sure that your desk is placed such that you are able to see the doorway.

You should select your furniture with your technology needs in mind. Smallish furniture doesn't accommodate the space required for a computer, printer, telephone/fax equipment, and so forth. Most businesspeople favor plentiful desk space and space designed for peripherals.

### Office Equipment and Supplies

The manner in which you equip your office contributes directly to your productivity. Fortunately, the costs of technology products such as computers, printers, scanners, and copy machines have reduced, making them more affordable. While the type of office equipment you'll need varies by business, Table 3.1 provides a list of the basic equipment most new businesses need.

*Table 3.1.  List of the Basic Equipment Most New Businesses Need*

| |
| --- |
| • Computer (desktop and laptop) |
| • Basic productivity software (such as Microsoft Office) |
| • Fax machine |
| • Laser printer (or color printer depending on your needs) |
| • Shredder |
| • Copier |
| • Scanner |
| • Fireproof safe |
| • Digital camera |
| • Landline phone with voicemail |
| • Smartphone |
| • Recycling bin |
| • Fire extinguisher |
| • First aid kit |

Carefully assess the equipment you need and buy good-quality equipment. Think through the type of work you'll be doing in your office and the types of transactions your business will conduct. For instance, if you'll be distributing purchase orders to customers, which they have to review and sign, you may need a fax machine for your clients to fax the orders back to you. The cost of a fax machine is a small price to pay to make it convenient for your customers to place orders. There are many multifunctional pieces of equipment on the market. If you select carefully, you may be able to buy a combination copier, printer, and fax machine that satisfies multiple needs. Keep the entirety of your needs in mind as you purchase equipment. For example, having a digital camera is handy to take pictures of clients using your products or company events to place in your newsletter or on your Web site.

There is specialized equipment that you may or may not need depending on your business. If you do a lot of mailing, a postage meter can save time. Similarly, a labeling machine is a near must if you'll be placing specialized labels on the products you sell.

Avoid paying full retail for equipment if you can help it. You can often obtain name-brand equipment through online platforms like eBay and Overstock.com for a reduced price. Think carefully before spending a lot on a piece of equipment that is only used occasionally. If you'll need to print color brochures occasionally, for example, it may be more cost-effective to utilize the FedEx store or a similar service than buy your own color printer. Rather than buying equipment, many vendors offer lease arrangements. You'll have to weigh the advantages and disadvantages of leasing rather than buying, but it may be an attractive alternative for some businesses.

In regard to office supplies, companies such as Staples and Office Depot offer credit accounts to small businesses. The accounts offer discounts and the ability to purchase online with next-day shipping or delivery. Maintain an adequate supply of pens, notepads, printer paper, paper clips, staplers, staples, and other office supplies.

## Communications Equipment and Software

It's becoming increasingly important for businesses to be equipped to effectively communicate with clients. This goes beyond basic equipment such as telephone, an internet connection, a fax machine, and an answering machine.

Many business owners now have a separate smartphone (like an Apple iPhone or an Android-equipped phone) to maintain their contact lists, call and text clients and employees, and take advantage of business-related apps. Online meeting services such as GoToMeeting (www.gotomeeting.com) allow businesses to make sales pitches or conduct meetings online. There are also services that allow small businesses to look larger than they are. For example, for as little as $12 per month, a business can access a service such as Grasshopper (http://grasshopper.com), which provides you a toll free number, unlimited extensions, and call forwarding to a mobile phone. How to select a phone system is covered in Chapter 6, Establishing a Professional Image.

## Step 4: Setting Up an Effective Filing System

Setting up an effective filing system is something that many businesses struggle with. There is no standard system. As a result, businesses often start with one system (like labeling files by subject) and when that doesn't work switch to another system (like labeling files numerically). It's also hard to decide where to store files. If you have an office that has a reception area where your assistant sits, and you both need access to the files, should they be stored in your office or in the area where your assistant sits? Similarly, if you have three salespersons, who have separate office and separate clients, should client files be stored in a central location, or should each salesperson store their own files? There are further complications. If important documents are exchanged with clients or vendors via e-mail, should the documents be stored on a computer, or should they be printed and stored in a permanent file?

There are no definitive answers to these questions. Each business will have to develop its own system. There are filing best practices, however, that will help you make the best choices. These are listed in Table 3.2.

## Table 3.2. Filing System Best Practices

| | |
|---|---|
| 1. | Pick a way to arrange your files and stick with it. Files can be arranged alphabetically, by subject, numerically, geographically, or chronologically. Most experts recommend that you arrange your files alphabetically. That way if you're looking for the file on Will Jones, who works in the Boulder, CO office of Google, you'll know immediately to look for the files labeled Jones, Will. You won't be looking for a file labeled Boulder, CO or a file labeled Google. You may have a separate file labeled Google, but it wouldn't contain the correspondence from Will Jones. |
| 2. | Separate your files into categories. Some businesses do this by having separate drawers for separate categories. Common categories include clients, prospects, invoices, bills, projects, personnel, and news clipping and articles. You can still file alphabetically; you're just separating your files into categories. |
| 3. | Color code your files: red for client files, blue for invoices, yellow for bills, green for projects, white for personnel, and tan for news clippings and articles. Which color goes with what category doesn't matter. The purpose is to make it easy to identify files. If you see a red file, you know it's a client file. |
| 4. | Don't try to force everything into hanging files. Consider having a separate location where you store oversized material such as product samples, brochures, photos, and catalogs. These items can be stored alphabetically in boxes or plastic containers. |
| 5. | Select your filing cabinets to accommodate your filing system, not the other way around. File cabinets can be vertical, lateral, or open shelf. The type of files cabinet you buy should be dictated by your needs and space. |
| 6. | Where you locate your files (within your office or suite of offices) is a judgment call. It may seem obvious to locate them nearest to the people who use them the most, but this isn't always the best answer. Some files, such as client files, may need to be where anyone can access them, without entering someone's private office. Files that contain private information, such as employee performance reviews, should be either locked (if in a common area) or placed in the founder or CEOs office. |
| 7. | Place material inside your files in a systematic manner. For example, all client files should have information arranged in the same order, so it's easy to quickly find a specific piece of information. |
| 8. | Avoid creating duplicate files. Some businesses try to solve the problem of whether a file should be in an individual employee's office or in a central location by creating two identical files. This approach rarely works. |
| 9. | Buy a filing labeling machine. |
| 10. | Purge your files regularly—at least once a year. |

## Step 5: Create Business Systems (From the Beginning)

It's extremely important that you start creating systems for how you'll operate your business. A system is a step-by-step process that you follow to complete a particular task so you get a specific (and consistent) outcome. Before scrambling to figure out how to do it each time you need something done, you must have a written checklist of steps that you can follow to complete a task. By creating systems, you can teach someone else to do what you do, then hand off the task so you can focus on more important things, such as making sales and servicing clients.

The following are examples of tasks that can be systemized:

- Processing orders
- Paying bills
- Paying employees
- Paying taxes
- Maintaining business licenses and permits
- Following up on sales leads
- Invoicing or billing customers
- Receiving inventory or stock.

For each task that you decide to systemize, you should create a checklist that documents the steps required to complete the task. It will take some trial and error. But over time, you should be able perfect each task to the point where it can be completed in a consistent manner regardless of whether it's being completed by you or an employee.

Your overarching goal is to create an "Operations Manual" for your business, which documents how things are done. Pick at least three tasks to organize into systems during the prelaunch stage of your First 100 Days plan, and have your Operations Manual started before your business launches.

A good illustration of the value of developing systems is systemizing how you maintain your business licenses and permits. If you're following the First 100 Days Plan outlined in the book, you've just been through the process of obtaining your business licenses and permits. Now, you should sit down and create a checklist for renewal of the licenses and permits you have. This checklist will document the process and save you the time of refreshing your memory on the steps to go through when the licenses and permits come up for renewal. "Maintaining Business Licenses and Permits" can be the first tab in your operations manual. You should also keep a master calendar (which covers this year and next year). You can now make your first entry on your master calendar, which will identify when you have to start the process of renewing your licenses and permits.

# APPENDIX

# First 100 Days Plan

## Prelaunch (Days 1–30)

### Part 3: Getting Up and Running

|  | Requirement | Check when done | Result (fill in below) |
|---|---|---|---|
| Step 1 | Choosing a Location | ☐ | Select a location for your business, and explain the rationale for your choice. It should be a physical location (such as 101 Oak Street, space in the Bank of American building on 5th and Main, or space in the strip mall on Washington and 23rd street). It has to be a real location. |
| Step 2 | Obtaining Insurance | ☐ | Describe the insurance you'd purchase for your business and the rationale for your choices. |
| Step 3 | Setting Up an Office | ☐ | Describe the office you'd set up for your business. Also describe the furniture you would place in the office, the equipment you would purchase or lease, and the communications hardware and software you would acquire. Include a budget. |

| | Requirement | Check when done | Result (fill in below) |
|---|---|---|---|
| Step 4 | Establishing a Filing System | ☐ | Describe the filing system you will use for your business. |
| Step 5 | Create business systems | ☐ | Describe three business systems you will create in the prelaunch stage of your business. |

# CHAPTER 4

# Bookkeeping and Financial Management

## Introduction

Another important prelaunch task is to establish your bookkeeping system and a financial management structure for your business. The main topics discussed in this section are shown later in the chapter. Again, the First 100 Days Plan focuses on the nuts-and-bolts aspects of starting a business, so the items discussed include the mechanics of setting up a business' financial management structure, rather than how to obtain financing. In particular, it's important for a business to have a good handle on its start-up costs and set up a bookkeeping system. It's also important to get up to speed on taxes and have a payroll system in place if you plan to hire employees.

| Step 1 | Setting Up a Bank Account and a Merchant Bank Account |
| Step 2 | Creating a Start-up Budget |
| Step 3 | Setting Up a Bookkeeping System |
| Step 4 | Getting Up to Speed on Business Taxes |
| Step 5 | Setting Up a Payroll System |
| Appendix | First 100 Days Plan: Bookkeeping and Setting Up a Business's Finances |

## Step 1: Setting Up a Bank Account and a Merchant Bank Account

It is important to set up a bank account for your business right away. Even if you're planning to operate as a sole proprietor, it's not a good practice to use your personal checking account to purchase business-related items, even if you keep track of record of which purchases are related to business.

If you're organized as a partnership, corporation, or an LLC, you must have a separate bank account.

If you plan to accept credit cards you'll need to set up a merchant account. A merchant account is a bank account that enables credit card networks to route money to your account. Virtually every bank offers merchant account services. The manner in which a merchant account works is shown in Table 4.1.

**Table 4.1. How a Merchant Account Works**

| | |
|---|---|
| 1. | Your customer presents you a credit card for payment, and you take the customer's credit card information. |
| 2. | The card is verified and approved (a service your merchant account company provides you). |
| 3. | Your merchant account provider passes the details to their credit card processor. |
| 4. | The credit card processor then debits the customer's credit card and deposits the money into your merchant credit card account. |
| 5. | Your merchant credit card account can be linked to your business checking account, so all monies are deposited and fees are withdrawn directly from your business checking account. |

You'll pay fees from 2% to 5% of the purchase price to accept credit cards, depending on the nature of your business. You should check several sources before settling on a merchant account provider. Fees vary from provider to provider. To get started, many banks charge an application fee and a setup fee to establish a merchant account. They then charge an annual fee along with the 2% to 5% they charge on processing credit cards for purchases.

Some businesses choose to not accept credit cards to avoid paying the merchant account fees. This is a judgment call on your part. If you'll be selling to customers that you invoice for payment, accepting credit cards can boost your cash flow by encouraging customers to pay you right away rather than asking you to wait 30 days or more for payment. The arrangement also works for your customer, because if they pay their credit card in full each month, they typically don't have to pay interest.

If you decide to accept credit cards and set up a merchant account, you'll need to purchase an electronic processor that automatically approves and records charges via a telephone line in your office, store, or business. The electronic processors cost about $200 each.

If you setup a merchant account through PayPal, you'll pay 2.9% of the purchase amount plus 30 cents per transaction. In some cases this is a cheaper option, but may be less convenient for your customers. There are new options for accepting credit cards that have been made possible as a result of mobile technologies, like smartphones. Square (www.square.com) offers merchant accounts that allow you to swipe your customer's credit cards using a reader that you plug into your smartphone. The reader is free. Square charges a flat 2.75% processing fee. It's a viable option for very small businesses, which may not want to pay the fees to open a traditional merchant account and buy the electronic processors. It's also a good option for service providers who go to people's homes, or businesses that sell at farmers markets or similar venues where using an electronic processor may not be practical.

## Step 2: Creating a Start-Up Budget

The first step in managing your business's money is to get a handle on what it will cost to launch the business. A start-up budget estimates the total cash that will be needed to get going. All businesses incur expenses before they make their first sale. A common mistake that business owners make is to underestimate their start-up costs and get caught short on cash before their business opens or during the early stages of operations.

### How to Calculate Your Start-Up Costs

To figure out your start-up budget you'll need to consider three categories of costs.

- Capital costs. This category includes real estate, buildings, equipment, vehicles, furniture, fixtures (shelves, wall brackets, cabinets), modifications to leased property, and similar capital purchases. These costs vary considerably depending on the business. A restaurant, retail, or manufacturing business may have substantial capital costs, while a home-based business may have little to no capital costs.

- One-Time Expenses. This category includes legal expenses, fees for business licenses and permits, deposit on a lease, deposits on utilities, setting up a merchant account, Web site design, designing a logo, and similar one-time expenses and fees. All businesses incur at least some of these expenses.

- Ramp-Up Expenses. Many businesses require a ramp-up period in which they lose money until they are fully up to speed and are profitable. For example, it usually takes a new fitness center several months to reach its membership goals. It's important to account for this period, and to have sufficient cash on hand to make it through. If you don't have a good idea of how much money you'll need, experts recommend that you set aside six months of your business's estimated monthly operating expenses to see you through the ramp-up period. You'll need to estimate your monthly expenses to arrive at that figure.

You may also need to set aside up to six months of living expenses for you and your family to see you through the ramp-up period. The need to do this depends on your individual situation. Some business owners have spouses who are working and can cover their living expenses. Other businesses start part-time, and the business owner keeps his or her full-time job until the business is profitable. Still other business owners have personal savings to draw on, or can draw on money provided by investors or a bank loan.

### Finding Information on Start-Up Costs

You need to estimate start-up costs as accurately as possible. There are several ways of finding the information you need, all of which involves a little legwork. You can estimate your expenses item by item by contacting the appropriate realtors, government agencies, vendors, service providers, and others who can provide informed estimates. For example, if you're thinking about leasing office space in one of several office complexes in your area, you can contact the properties directly to gather information on their rental rates. Another way to identify start-up costs is to talk to the owners of businesses that are similar to the one you're planning to start. You should try to find businesses that are outside your trade area so the owners don't see you as a potential competitor. Another approach is to contact a trade association that represents businesses in the industry you'll be entering. Many trade associations compile statistics on start-up costs. There are also online forums that are potentially helpful. A good place to start is the Small Business Ideas Forum (www.smallbusinessbrief.com). You can start a discussion thread on any small-business-related topic that you want and can normally obtain good-quality advice from other small business people who participate in the forum.

### Determining the Financing You'll Need (If Applicable)

One you know what your start-up costs will be, you'll be in a position to determine if you can swing it on your own, or if you'll need to pursue outside financing. Five ways to finance a new business include (a) personal funds, including loans from friends and family and bootstrapping, (b) debt financing, (c) equity funding, (d) grants, and (e) other potential sources of financing, such as crowd sourcing platforms such as Kickstarter (www.kickstarter.com) and Indiegogo (www.indiegogo.com), and vendor credit. There are many excellent Web sites and books that focus on the topic of raising money for start-ups.

## Step 3: Setting Up a Bookkeeping System

An important step in the prelaunch stage of a business is to set up a proper bookkeeping system. Most new business owners tackle this challenge themselves, but there are other options. There are many bookkeeping services that will maintain your books for you for a fee. If you're opening a business that will process dozens or hundreds of transactions a day, such as a restaurant or retail store, you might want to consider a professional bookkeeping service or hiring a part-time or full-time employee to keep your books. If you plan to do the bookkeeping yourself, an important recommendation is to seek out an accountant or professional bookkeeper and schedule a consulting session. An experienced accountant or bookkeeper can help you get off on the right track, and can make recommendations based on your specific business.

Fortunately, there software packages that are easy to learn and use that simplify bookkeeping and financial management tasks. Programs such as QuickBooks have several different versions to meet the needs of all types and sizes of businesses. Select one of these programs and use it. Don't keep your books by hand. It's just too time consuming and prone to error. In addition, by doing it by hand it's much more difficult to produce the types of useful financial reports and forecasts that a program like QuickBooks generates.

### Initial Calls—Tax Year Selection and Cash Method Versus Accrual Method of Accounting

There are two decisions that you'll have to make early on that will affect how you keep your books. The first is your tax year. For most businesses the tax year will be the same as the calendar year. If you're organizing as a C corporation, you have more flexibility, and you should check with an attorney or accountant to see what would be the best choice for you. The second call is whether to use the cash method or accrual method of accounting. It's an important call, because once you make the decision, you can't change it without the permission from the Internal Revenue Service (IRS). It's beyond the scope of this book to fully describe the pluses and minuses of cash basis versus accrual basis accounting. A consulting session with an accountant or professional bookkeeper can help you make the decision.

In short, the difference between the cash method and the accrual method of accounting concerns the timing of when transactions, both sales and purchases, are either credited to or debited from your accounts. Under the cash method, income is counted when cash (or a check) is actually received, and not necessarily when the sale occurs. Expenses are counted when they are actually paid, and not when you make the purchase. As a result, if you placed an order with a supplier for $2,000 in supplies in December but you didn't pay the invoice until January, the expense would be recorded in January rather than in December. Under the accrual method, both sales and purchase transactions are counted when they occur, regardless of when the money is actually received or paid. So in the previous example, the $2,000 in supplies would be counted as an expense in December rather than in January even if the supplies weren't delivered until January. The most significant impact of your choice of accounting methods reflects on your taxes. If you choose the accrual method and place an order in December 2012 but don't pay for it until January 2013, you must show the expense on your 2012 tax returns, you can't shift it to your 2013 tax returns.

Most new businesses choose the cash method of accounting. The general rule is that if you have inventories (such as a retail or manufacturing business), you must use the accrual method. But businesses are generally free to choose if they have sales of less than $1 million per year, which captures most businesses. Again, you should consult with an accountant or professional bookkeeper to make the right decision for your business.

### Basics of Keeping Books

At a basic level, keeping books involves three steps: keeping records, entering information into a bookkeeping system, and generating financial reports, as shown in Figure 4.1. The following is a brief description of each step.

*Keeping Records.* The process starts with carefully keeping records of all your income and expenses. Each transaction must be backed up by some type of record, such as an invoice or a receipt. The best way to handle this is to create a system for recording and filing the documentation (as recommended in Chapter 3, Getting Up and Running). You should never have to search for a sales or expense receipt. They should be filed in a consistent manner where you or an authorized employee can easily find them.

The method you'll use to keep records will depend largely on the nature of your business. It can range from simple files labeled "income receipts" and "expense receipts" if your business is small and you don't

*Figure 4.1. Three steps involved in keeping books.*

have a large number of transactions to a sophisticated cash register-based point-of-sale system.

There are certain rules of thumb associated with handling income receipts. Income receipts should always include the date, the amount, a brief description of what was sold, an indication of how payment was made (cash, credit card, check), whether the sale was subject to sales tax, and the amount of the sales tax if applicable. It's critical that you separate out sales tax so you can accurately pass on the sales tax revenue to state tax authorities. You should also document any funds coming into the business that are not related to sales, such as money from a loan or money you're putting in from your personal accounts. All loans, whether your own or from a bank, should be associated with a promissory note. For tax purposes, you need to clearly distinguish money that comes in from sales from that which comes in from non-sales-related activities. Income from sales is taxable (minus expenses) while income from non-sales-related activities is not.

There are also rules of thumb associated with expense receipts. Again, each receipt should include data, the amount, the method of payment, who was paid, and a description of what type of expense it was (i.e., payroll, rent, supplies, advertising, utilities). It's important to be as accurate as possible in labeling expenses because when you enter them into a bookkeeping software program you'll have to place them in categories.

*Entering Information into a Bookkeeping System.* Next, on a periodic basis (every Friday afternoon, for example), you should enter your income and expense receipts into a bookkeeping software system (before computers, people entered income and receipts into hardbound books called ledgers). Along with traditional boxed software products, like Quickbooks and Sage 50, there is also online small business accounting services (called software as a service) such as WorkingPoint.com.

It takes time to learn how to use a bookkeeping software program, so don't wait until your business launches to start. At a minimum, you'll have expense items to input before your launch date. The key is to enter your transactions correctly, so focus on that component from the beginning. If your transactions are entered correctly, the program automatically generates the majority of the reports.

When you setup your program, you'll be first asked (in most cases) to set up accounts, such as checking accounts, saving accounts, and a credit card accounts. In some instances, you'll also set up accounts labeled "accounts receivable" and "accounts payable." The next thing you'll be asked to do is to create income and expense categories. This is where your business may vary significantly from another business owner. Your income and expense categories will reflect the nature of your business. You'll be alerted to the fact that different types of income and expenses are treated differently for tax purposes, so it's essential that they are tracked separately in your bookkeeping system. Table 4.2 provides a list of typical income and expense categories.

*Table 4.2. Typical Income and Expense Categories in Small Business Bookkeeping Systems*

| Income categories | Expense categories |
|---|---|
| Taxable sales | Payroll |
| Sales tax | Rent |
| Nontaxable sales | Utilities |
| Loans | Travel |
| Contributions from investors | Office supplies |
| Grants | Smartphone expenses |

The way you set up your categories is important beyond getting it right for tax purposes. By seeing where your income is coming from each month, and looking at the amounts in your individual expense categories, you can usually make better financial and strategic decisions.

*Generating Financial Reports.* Your bookkeeping system will enable you to generate a number of financial reports, including profit and loss statements, cash flow projections, and balance sheets. You'll also be able to generate breakdowns of income and expense items in a number of different ways.

### Additional Notes

Three additional notes regarding setting up a bookkeeping system: first, if your business is specialized, like you're opening a veterinarian practice or you're becoming a building contractor, there may be specialized bookkeeping software programs designed specifically for your industry. If this is the case, it may be worth checking out. Second, Quickbooks (made by Intuit) is by far the most popular small business bookkeeping software. An advantage of Quickbooks is that there are many tutorials available to help you learn Quickbooks, and many of your peer business owners will be using Quickbooks, so it isn't difficult to find someone to answer questions. QuickBooks also sells many add-on products, such as industry-specific applications to help you manage a certain type of businesses. Finally, there are merits to doing your books yourself initially, even if you can afford a bookkeeping service. People who do their own books are typically "closer" to their finances than people who don't—which means they gain a better "feel" for where their money is coming from and where it is going. Having a good feel for your finances can be critical in the early stages of a business.

## Step 4: Getting Up to Speed on Business Taxes

It's important to get up to speed quickly on business taxes. It's a nuts-and-bolts issue that you have to study and comply with. Even if you're not earning revenue, you still need to know about taxes.

Most business owners have their taxes prepared by a professional tax preparer, or use a software program such as TurboTax. Quickbooks data can be imported directly into TurboTax. Even if you have a professional preparer do your taxes, you should still become familiar with business tax issues. You need to understand your tax forms and be able to explain withholding requirements to your employees.

In general, businesses are subject to taxes at three levels: federal taxes, state taxes, and country and city taxes. A discussion of each subsequently follows.

### Federal Taxes

The federal government, via the IRS, levies the following taxes on small businesses and their owners:

- Federal Income Tax
- Federal Payroll Taxes
- Self-Employment Tax

*Federal Income Tax.* If you're a sole proprietor, your business doesn't pay taxes. Instead, you report your business income or loss on Schedule C, and file it with your personal income tax return. Similarly, if you're a general partnership, your business doesn't pay taxes. You file an informational tax form (Form 1065), which tells the IRS how much each partner earned. Each partner then reports his or share of the income or loss on Schedule E, and files it with their personal tax income return. If you're a subchapter S corporation, the corporation itself does not pay taxes. You file Form 1120-S, which is an informational return, telling the IRS how much each shareholder made. Each shareholder is then required to show their portion of the income or loss and report it on Schedule E of their individual tax return.

If you're a C corporation, the corporation *does* file a tax return and pay income on its earnings. The owners are then required to pay income tax on their share of the dividend income paid by the corporation (thus, double taxation). From a practical standpoint, most small C corporations either pay out their earnings to their shareholders in the form of salaries and bonuses, or reinvest their profits in the business. Of course, their shareholders will have to pay taxes on their salaries and bonuses, but the double taxation whammy rarely kicks in.

Finally, if you're a limited liability company (LLC), and it's a single-member LLC, you'll report the income (or loss) from your business on Schedule C and file it with your federal tax return. An LLC with two or more members doesn't pay taxes. Instead, it files an informational return (Form 1065) telling the IRS how much each member made. Each member must then report his or her share of the income (or loss) on Schedule E and file it with their individual tax return.

*Federal Payroll Taxes.* There are three forms of federal payroll taxes that apply to businesses having employees. First, you must withhold income taxes from your employee's paychecks. IRS Publication 15, Circular E, *Employer's Tax Guide*, explains how to do this, along with other employer federal tax responsibilities. The publication can be obtained at www.irs.gov by simply typing "IRS Publication 15, Circular E" into the search box. In short, the withholding amount is determined by the employee's filing status (single, married, or married but withholding at the higher single rate), the number of dependents, and the amount of the employee's salary. Employees declare their number of dependents on Form W-4.

The second form of federal payroll taxes is Social Security (FICA) and Medicare. You must withhold the employee's share of Social Security tax and Medicare tax from the employee's paycheck. You must also pay the employer's share. The amounts to be withheld are listed in the most current version of IRS Publication 15, Circular E (described earlier). At the time this chapter was written (June 2012), employers were required to withhold 4.2% of their employees' wages for Social Security (up to $110,100 in income) and 1.45% of wages for Medicare. The employers share was 6.2% of wages for Social Security and 1.45% for Medicare.

The third form of federal payroll taxes is Federal Unemployment Tax (FUTA). The employer is responsible for paying this tax—it is not withheld from the employee's paycheck. The Federal Unemployment Tax rate is 6.2% of the first $7,000 of the employee's wages for the year, and is reported on Form 940 or 940EZ. You'll need to check with a tax advisor to see the rate that applies to you. Employers are given a credit for participating in state unemployment programs. The credit reduces the rate to 0.8% of the first $7,000 of the employee's wages for most employers.

*Federal Self-Employment Tax.* If you are operating as a sole proprietor or a partner (in a partnership), you must pay federal self-employment tax along with income tax on the income you receive. The self-employment tax is equal to the employer's and the employee's portion of the Social Security and Medicare taxes that you and your employer would pay on your wages if you received it as an employee.

Currently, the self-employment tax is 13.3% on income up to $106,800 and 2.9% for income beyond that. You report your self-employment tax on Schedule SE, which is included with your personal tax return. Computing your self-employment tax gets a little complicated if you still have a job that's subject to withholding. The income from your job will reduce the tax base for your self-employment tax. See a tax advisor or study the IRS instruction booklet for Form SE, which is available at www.irs.gov.

### State Taxes

States typically levy the following taxes on small businesses and their owners:

- State Income Tax
- State Payroll Tax (primarily withholding for unemployment insurance)
- Special Taxes.

State income taxes are levied in much the same way as federal income taxes. You should check with your tax preparer or local tax authorities to determine the specifics for your state. There are a handful of states that do not have state income tax, including Alaska, New Hampshire, Tennessee, Florida, South Dakota, Washington, Nevada, Texas, and Wyoming. One of the benefits of not having a state income tax is that it makes the state more attractive for businesses.

Payroll taxes are collected at the state level in some states, primarily for state unemployment insurance. In Oklahoma, for example, the withholding rate is 1.2% for the first $18,600 in income (as of June, 2012).

Some states levy special taxes on certain types of business activities such as selling gasoline, cigarettes, or alcohol. Some states also collect taxes on LLCs and limited partnerships.

Businesses are required to collect sales tax on goods and some services from their customers, as explained in Chapter 2, Legal Requirements Part 2, and touched on earlier in this chapter. Once the taxes are collected, they're passed on to state tax authorities. The state tax authorities typically collect the sales tax for both state and local sales tax assessments.

You also need to check with your state and local governments to see if you need a special state or local ID to process taxes.

### County and City Taxes

County and city governments vary in terms of the taxes they impose. Property taxes are levied primarily at the county level, and apply to businesses that own real estate. Some county and city governments impose a small sales tax, which businesses must collect and submit along with the state-imposed sales tax to the state tax authorities, as explained earlier.

Cities and counties vary in terms of how often the business licenses and permits they issue must be renewed, which is a form of a tax. In San Francisco, CA, for example, a person or company conducting business in the city must maintain a business license and renew it every year. The license costs between $25 and $500 per year, depending on the business's estimated payroll (the vast majority of business pay between $25 and $150 a year).

City and county governments levy other taxes, which are unique to individual locations. Check with your local tax authorities before you launch your business to see what taxes apply to your business.

### Deductions

It's helpful to know a little about business deductions. Obviously, you want as many deductions as you can to minimize your federal and state income tax obligations.

There are two categories of deductions: current expenses and capital expenses. Current expenses are everyday expenses that are deducted from your current income. The IRS states that "ordinary and necessary" business expenses can be subtracted from your business income for federal tax purposes. Ordinary and necessary expenses include rent, supplies, business insurance, payroll, utility bills, advertising expenses, and so forth, and are fully deductible.

In contrast, capital expenditures are not fully deductible right away. A capital expense is for an item that has a useful life of more than a year, such as a vehicle, a piece of machinery, or real estate. Capital items must be depreciated, which means that the deduction is spread out over several years. Depreciation rules are explained in IRS Publication 946, *How to Depreciate Property*, available at www.irs.gov.

There are special rules for deducting the start-up costs of a business. In short, you can deduct up to $5,000 of your start-up costs in the first year of business. If your start-up costs exceed $5,000, you can deduct the excess amount in equal installments over the next 15 years.

### When Taxes Are Due

You should pay particular attention to the time when the various taxes referred previously are due. Failure to pay taxes on time can result in penalties and other negative consequences. Once your business gets rolling, you'll have to pay your federal- and state-estimated income taxes on a quarterly basis. Check with your tax authorities to see when your other taxes are due. Make sure to follow the rules closely if you have to collect sales tax and remit them as instructed to your state tax authorities.

## Step 5: Setting Up a Payroll System

When you start hiring employees, you'll have to set up a payroll system. This is something you have to do correctly. Not only do you want to pay your employees on time, but you also need to make sure all the deductions are withdrawn from your employee's paychecks correctly.

Table 4.3 describes the steps in setting up a payroll system.

### *Table 4.3. Steps to Setting Up a Payroll System*

| | |
|---|---|
| 1. | Obtain an FEIN. Obtain a Federal Employer Identification Number (FEIN) if you don't already have one. |
| 2. | Obtain necessary state/local IDs. Some state and local governments require businesses to obtain ID numbers in order to process taxes. |
| 3. | Independent Contractor or Employee. Make sure to identify each person who works for you as either an independent contractor or an employee. It makes a difference how you pay them. |
| 4. | Take Care of Employee Paperwork. New employees must fill out Federal Income Tax Withholding Form W-4, and return it to you. |
| 5. | Decide on a Pay Period. Set up a pay period. In some states, pay periods are set by state law. The most common pay periods are monthly or bimonthly. |
| 6. | Document Your Employee Compensation Terms. This includes how you'll track employee hours, how you handle paid time off, how an employee accumulates sick leave and vacation time, and so forth. Also, you'll need to deduct from your employee's paychecks not only the applicable tax withholdings but also health insurance premiums, retirement contributions, and other voluntary contributions. |
| 7. | Choosing a Payroll System. You'll need to decide whether to process payroll in-house or whether to use an outsource provider, such as Paychex. It is worth doing research to investigate the pluses and minuses of each option. |
| 8. | Running Payroll. One you have collected all your forms and information, you can start running your payroll (or turn information over to your outsource firm provided to run it). |
| 9. | Keep Good Records. Federal and some state laws require that employers keep certain records for specified periods of time. |
| 10. | Report Payroll Taxes. There are several payroll tax reports that you are required to submit to the appropriate authorities on either a quarterly or an annual basis. |

*Source:* SBA.gov, www.sba.gov, "10 Steps to Setting Up a Payroll System," Accessed on June 5, 2012.

# APPENDIX
# First 100 Days Plan

## Prelaunch (Days 1–30)

### Part 4: Bookkeeping and Setting Up a Business's Finances

|  | Requirement | Check when done | Result (fill in below) |
|---|---|---|---|
| Step 1 | Setting up a Bank Account and a Merchant Bank Account | ☐ | Identify the bank where you will set up your business bank account. If applicable, identify the bank where you'll set up your merchant bank account. Report the steps necessary to set up a merchant bank account at the bank you've chosen, and what the fees will be. |
| Step 2 | Creating a Start-up Budget | ☐ | Create a start-up budget for your business. |
| Step 3 | Setting up a Bookkeeping System | ☐ | Identify the tax year you would use and whether you'd use the cash method or the accrual method of accounting. Identify and describe the bookkeeping system you'll use for your business. Identify the major categories of income and expenses that you'll setup in the system. |
| Step 4 | Getting up to Speed on Business Taxes | ☐ | If you plan to have employees, describe the taxes you'll have to withhold from your employees' paychecks. Identify the federal, state, and local taxes that your business will have to pay. If you'll be subject to self-employment taxes, describe how you'd figure your self-employment tax liability. |

*(Continued)*

## Part 4: Bookkeeping and Setting Up a Business's Finances (Continued)

|  | Requirement | Check when done | Result (fill in below) |
|---|---|---|---|
| Step 5 | Setting up a Payroll System | ☐ | If you plan to have employees, determine whether you'd process your payroll in-house or use an outsource provider. If you plan to use an outsource provider, identify the company you'd plan to use, and briefly describe how their process works. |

# CHAPTER 5

# Protecting Your Intellectual Property

## Introduction

Imagine that you have started a business to produce a new type of portable heating and cooling device for homes and offices. It's unique in that it is able to maintain a constant room temperature—by emitting hot air when the room is too cold and emitting cold air when the room is too hot. You've name the device "Constant Comfort Air Handler." Your tagline is "Always the same temperature, always the same comfort." You have just acquired the Internet domain name www.constantcomfortair handler.com.

You recognize that you own some intellectual property, so you go to an attorney for advice. Over the next several weeks, the attorney helps you apply for a utility patent on the device itself, a trademark for the "Constant Comfort Air Handler" name, and copyright protection for an infomercial you have produced to promote your product. You have also designated certain portion of what you do as trade secrets. For example, the software code that allows your device to seamlessly switch from emitting hot air to cold air is not protected by a patent. It's nearly impossible for a competitor to learn the code by reverse-engineering one of your devices. As a result, rather than disclosing this information, which would be necessary if you patented it, you have decided to keep it secret and protect it internally.

Similar to Constant Comfort Air Handler, many new businesses have valuable intellectual property. Intellectual property is any product of human intellect that is intangible but has value in the marketplace. Historically, businesses have thought of their physical assets—the brick and mortar—as their most important assets. Increasingly, however, a business's intellectual assets are the most valuable. Think of the value of the iPhone trade name, the Nike "swoosh" logo, or Dropbox's unique way of storing computer files. All of these are examples of intellectual property that provides their respective businesses a competitive advantage in the marketplace.

This chapter contains a heads-up on the intellectual property that a new business should protect before it launches. In most cases you won't have all of your intellectual property developed prior to launch, so it's an issue you'll want to revisit periodically. But most businesses will have a name, a logo, and some printed material prior to launch. It's important to make it a priority to protect this material in the prelaunch phase of your First 100 Days Plan.

Note of caution. Many businesses launch with a false sense of security regarding portions of their intellectual property, such as their business's name. For example, if you've filed documents to form a business entity, such as a subchapter S corporation or an LLC, you were asked to identify your business's name, and if no other company in your state was using the name, the state likely authorized you to use it. However, a state's authorization to form a business with a particular name does not also give you trademark protection for the name. That can only be accomplished through the United States Patent & Trademark Office (USPTO). If a business in another state was using the same name, it could potentially stop you from using your name if it felt you were interfering with its trademark.

The four forms of intellectual property protection are patents, copyrights, trademarks, and trade secrets.

| Step 1 | Patents |
|--------|---------|
| Step 2 | Copyrights |
| Step 3 | Trademarks |
| Step 4 | Trade Secrets |
| Appendix | First 100 Days Plan: Protecting Your Intellectual Property |

## Step 1: Patents

There are three types of patents: utility patents, design patents, and plant patents. In most cases, patents are filed to protect new products, such as the Constant Comfort Air Handler. If you're starting a business like a service business and it looks like patents won't apply, you should familiarize yourself with patent law anyway. Sometimes businesses that typically don't apply for patents over time develop a process or capability that is patentable. An example would be a hairstyling salon that develops a unique software product for scheduling consults and appointments. While the hairstyling salon itself may be doing nothing that is patentable, the software product may be patentable, and may produce significant licensing income if properly marketed and legally protected.

If you are creating an original new product, it's important that you become familiar with patent law right away. If you're not familiar with how and when patent applications should be filed, you might unwittingly forfeit your right to apply for a patent.

There are three topics to consider regarding patents in the prelaunch phase of the First 100 Days Plan: what is a patent and what's eligible for patent protection; the need for urgency in filing your patent application; and the process of obtaining a patent.

### What Is a Patent and What Is Eligible for Patent Protection

A patent is a grant from the federal government conferring the rights to exclude others from making, selling, or using an invention during the term of the patent. A patent does not give its owner the right to make, use, or sell the invention; it gives the owner only the right to exclude others from doing so. This is a confusing issue. If a business is granted a patent for an item, it is natural to assume that it could start making and selling the item immediately. But it cannot. A patent owner can legally make or sell the invention only if no other patents are infringed upon by doing so. For example, if the inventor of the Constant Comfort Air Handler obtained a patent on the device, and the device needed technology patented earlier by GE to work, the inventor would need permission from GE to make and sell the device. GE many refuse permission or ask for a licensing fee for the use of its patented technology (called "prior art" in patent terminology). Although this system may seem odd, it is really the only way the system could work. Many inventions are improvements on existing inventions, and the system allows for improvements to be patented, but only with the permission of the original inventors, who usually benefit by obtaining licensing income in exchange for their consent.

There are three types of patents: utility patents, design patents, and plant patents. Utility patents are the most common type of patent and cover what we normally think of as new inventions. The term of a utility patent is 20 years from the date of the initial application. A patent is not renewable. After 20 years, the invention falls into the public domain. There are three basic requirements for a patent to be granted. The subject of the patent application must be (a) useful, (b) novel in relation to prior art in the field, and (c) not obvious to a person of ordinary skill in the field.

### The Need for Urgency in Filing Your Patent Application

There are two reasons why it's important to have a sense of urgency in regard to filing a patent application. First, a patent must be applied for within 1 year of a product or process being first offered for sale, put into public use, or described in any printed publication—or the right to file a patent application is forfeited. Second, the United States historically has had a "first to invent" standard for those who have the right to file a patent application. The standard meant that the first person to invent a new product or process had priority in terms of patent rights, regardless of the order in which competing inventors file their patent applications. On March 16, 2013 the United States will switch to a "first to file" standard, meaning the first person to file a patent application for a particular product or process has priority. This switch increases the pressure to file earlier rather than later if you've invented a new product.

There are reasons to wait on filing a patent application, which are beyond the scope of this book. The reasons relate to strengthening the "claims" in a patent application prior to filing the application. This is an issue you'll discuss with your patent attorney if applicable.

One provision of patent law that's particularly important for new business owners is that the U.S. Patent and Trademark Office allows inventors to file a provisional patent application. A provisional patent application allows an inventor to establish a "priority" filing date for an invention for up to 1 year, pending the filing of a complete and final application. It also allows the term "Patent Pending" to be applied to an invention.

### The Process for Obtaining a Patent

Obtaining a patent is a lengthy process. The U.S. Patent and Trademark Office is backlogged, and it currently takes upward of 3 years to obtain a patent. Attorney's fees for filing a patent application vary depending on the complexity of the patent, from as little as $5,000 for a simple device, like a new type of coat hanger or a bottle opener, to $25,000 and up for a complex invention. There are also filing fees involved.

Before you retain a patent attorney, you can do your own search to get a sense of whether a product you've invented or in the process of developing is patentable. You can do this by accessing the United State Patent & Trademark Office (USPTO) Web site (www.uspto.gov) and conducting a preliminary search. An even simpler-to-use patent search tool is available via Google at www.google.com/patents. What you're looking for is whether someone has already patented the device you're thinking about building. If they have, then it not only tells you that your device is not patentable, but that you should also check with a patent attorney to make sure you won't be infringing on someone else's patent if you move forward.

If you decide to apply for a provisional patent application or a full-utility patent, it is highly recommended to you work with a patent attorney. As an indication of the difficulty of writing a patent application, the USPTO requires all attorneys and agents to pass a tough exam before they can interact with the agency on behalf of a client. Even though there are "patent-it-yourself" books and Web sites on the market, it is generally naïve for a business owner to think that the patent process can be successfully navigated without expert help.

## Step 2: Copyrights

A copyright is a form of intellectual property that grants to the owner of a work of authorship the legal right to determine how the work is used and to obtain the economic benefits from it. The work must be in a tangible form, such as a brochure or an advertising copy, or must be saved in an electronic format. A work does not have to have artistic merit to be eligible for copyright protection. As a result, an operating manual or an advertising pamphlet qualifies for protection.

There are three things you need to know about copyrights in the prelaunch stage of your business: what is protected by a copyright, how to obtain a copyright, and when you should make the effort to copyright.

### What Is Protected by a Copyright?

The primary categories of material that can be copyrighted are shown in Table 5.1.

**Table 5.1. Categories of Material That Can be Copyrighted**

| | |
|---|---|
| • Literary works | • Software |
| • Musical compositions | • Graphic designs |
| • Sound recordings | • Videos |
| • Drawings | • Photos |
| • Artwork | • Poems |
| • Podcasts | • Original authorship appearing on a Web site |

Anything that is written down is a literary work. Characters, such as the Aflac duck or the GEICO gecko, can be copyrighted. Derivative works, which are works that are new renditions of something that is already copyrighted, are also copyrightable. As a result of this provision, a musician who performs a rendition of a song copyrighted by Beyonce can obtain a copyright on her effort. Of course, Beyonce (or whoever she has assigned her copyrights to) would have to agree to the infringement on her copyright of the original song before the new song could be used commercially, which is a common method that composers and bands earn extra income.

### How to Obtain a Copyright?

Technically, a copyright exists the moment a work of authorship assumes a tangible form. You can enhance copyright protection by attaching the copyright notice, or copyright bug as it is called. The bug—a C inside a circle—typically appears in the following form: © 2013 Constant Comfort Air Handler Inc. By placing this notice at the bottom of an advertising brochure, in the credits at the end of a video, or toward the bottom of a digital photo, the author (or the company) can prevent others from copying the work without permission and claiming that they did not know that the work was copyrighted. Substitutions for the copyright bug include the word Copyright and the abbreviation Copr.

You can also enhance your protection by registering your work with the U.S. Copyright Office (www.copyright.gov). Registration is voluntary. You have to register your work with the U.S. Copyright Office, which costs $35, to win damages in an infringement lawsuit. Copyrights last for a long time. Any work created on or after January 1, 1978, is protected for the life of the author plus 70 years.

### *When You Should Make the Effort to Copyright?*

There are two categories of original authorship that should be copyrighted from the inception of your business. First, you should make a habit of attaching the copyright bug to all original print and electronic materials that will be seen by the public. This includes marketing brochures, print ads, digital photos, videos, menus (if your business is a restaurant), and so forth. A copyright protects you from someone using your work without permission. You should also place the copyright bug on internal documents, such as forms you develop and your operations manual. These documents may also be treated as trade secrets, but placing the copyright bug on them provides you a double layer of protection.

Second, if you're producing a material that falls into one of the categories shown in Table 5.1, and it has commercial potential, it should be copyrighted. For example, if you own a bicycle shop and create a directory of the Top 100 bike trails in your state, and offer the directory for sale, it should be copyrighted and the copyright should be registered with the U.S. Copyright Office. Similarly, if you're a freelance writer or a photographer, you should copyright the content you create. In most instances, affixing the copyright bug will be sufficient. When you sell the material you created, you'll be asked to transfer the copyright to the items you sell to parties you sell them to.

# Step 3: Trademarks

A trademark is any word, name, symbol, or design used to identify the source or origin of products or services and to distinguish those products or services from others. A service mark identifies the sources of a service rather than goods. The term "trademark" is used to refer to both trademarks and service marks. At a minimum, all new businesses should obtain trademark protection on their name and, in many instances, other words or symbols associated with their business or products. There are three things that a new business owner needs to know about trademarks: what can be trademarked, rules of thumb for selecting or creating appropriate trademarks, and how a trademark is obtained.

### What Can be Trademarked?

Table 5.2 provides a list of items that are eligible for trademark protection. As shown, trademark protection is broad, and provides many opportunities for businesses to differentiate themselves from one another.

*Table 5.2. Items Eligible for Trademark Protection*

| | |
|---|---|
| • Words—such as Constant Comfort Air Handler. | • Designs and logos—such as the McDonald's Golden Arches. |
| • Numbers and letters—such as 3M, CNN, and 1-800-FLOWERS. | • Sounds—such as the familiar four-tone sound that accompanies "Intel Inside" commercials. |
| • Trade dress—such as the distinctive appearance of the inside of a Panera Bread restaurant. | • Fragrances—such as special scent on certain brands of stationary. |
| • Shapes—such as the distinctive shape of the Apple iPhone. | • Colors—such as the distinctive purple color of Nexium, a pill that treats acid reflux disease (advertised as the "purple pill"). |

### Rules of Thumb for Selecting or Creating Appropriate Trademarks

There are three rules of thumb for selecting trademarks. First, similar to selecting the name for a business, you cannot select or create a trademark that is confusingly similar to a trademark already in use. As a result, if you create a logo that resembles the familiar Apple logo, Apple will probably object and prevail. Second, words or images that create favorable impressions of a product or service are helpful. For example, a name such as Safe and Secure Childcare positively resonates with parents. Finally, a mark, whether it is a name, logo, or distinctive color, should display creativity and strength. Similar to selecting a name for a business (and in many cases it will be the name of your business) it should also be a word or phrase that is easy to remember, spell, and pronounce.

### How Is a Trademark Obtained?

Trademarks are obtained through the United State Patent & Trademark Office (USPTO) and are renewable every 10 years, as long as the mark remains in use. An application for a trademark can be filed directly through the USPTO Web site at (www.uspto.gov/teas) or you can utilize a service such as LegalZoom (www.legalzoom.com) or Rocket Lawyer (www.rocketlawyer.com) to do it for you. You can also hire an attorney to guide you through the process. The filing fee is $325 or $275 depending on how you file (it's cheaper to file electronically). If you're filing for protection of a design of logo, if must be in .jpg format and follow the filing instructions on the USPTO Web site.

Prior to filing for trademark protection, you should conduct a search to see if your trademark has already been taken or is it confusingly similar to a mark already in use. If you find that it is, then you've saved yourself the trouble and expense of being turned down by the USPTO. The USPTO's Web site provides a powerful trademark search engine at www.uspto.gov/trademarks. There is a catch. The USPTO's search engine only searches trademarks that are registered. In the United States, you are not required to register a mark to obtain protection. A trademark attorney can perform a more comprehensive search for you if you think it's necessary.

Technically, a trademark does not need to be registered to receive protection and to prevent other companies from using confusingly similar marks. Once a mark is used in commerce, such as in an advertisement, it is protected. There are several advantages, however, to registering a trademark with the USPTO. Registered marks are:

- allowed to use the federal trademark symbol (®);
- listed in the USPTO's online databases;
- provide the ability to bring action for infringement concerning the mark in federal court.

The right to use the federal trademark symbol is particularly important. Attaching the trademark symbol to a product (such as Constant Comfort Air Handler (®)) provides notice of a trademark owner's protection.

When you apply for a trademark you'll be asked to designate whether your application is a "use-in-commerce" application or an "intent-to-use" application. The difference is whether you've actually used the mark. If you haven't, you'll file under "intent-to-use," which is based on a *good faith* intent to use the mark in commerce. If you have used the mark, you'll file under "use-in-commerce" and there is no additional fee.

Unlike Internet domain names, people can't register trademarks and then "sit" on them with the intention of selling them to new businesses that would want to use the name. If you register a trademark, you have to either use it in commerce or attest to the fact that you plan to use it in commerce soon. As part of your application for a mark, you'll be asked to file a specimen, which is a rendition of how the mark will be used in association with the product or service you're selling. For example, if the owners of Constant Comfort Air Handler designed a logo for the product, and applied for trademark protection on the logo, they'd had to provide a specimen of how the logo will be used. If it will be displayed on the bottom right-hand corner of the device, a digital photo of the finished device with the logo visible would qualify as a specimen.

It takes up to a year to get a trademark application approved. Once you file an application, however, somebody cannot claim the same mark if their filing date is later than yours. Once you have obtained a trademark, you must "maintain" it. You must file your first maintenance document between the fifth and sixth year after the registration date and other maintenance documents thereafter.

The most common reason that trademarks application is denied is that the mark (or name) you're applying for has already been trademarked or is confusingly similar to a mark already in use, as discussed earlier. There are also notable exceptions to trademark protection. You cannot trademark deceptive marks (e.g., you can't trademark the phrase "Fresh Washington Apples" if the apples aren't from Washington), descriptive marks (you can't design a new type of soccer ball and trademark the name "soccer ball"), or surnames (e.g., if your name is Rebecca Smith, you can't trademark the name Smith. If you combine your name with the name of a business, such as "Smith's Fresh Seafood," then that name can be trademarked).

The USPTO will answer questions about trademark registration at 1-800-786-9199. There are also instructional videos for first-time filers at www.uspto.gov/trademarks.

## Step 4: Trade Secrets

Most businesses, including start-ups, have information that is critical to their success but does not qualify for patent, copyright, or trademark protection. Some of this information needs to be kept secret to help a business maintain a competitive advantage. An example is a business's business plan. The founder or founders of a business may have worked extremely hard on the plan, and if it fell into the hands of a competitor, its value would be diminished. A document such as a business plan should be guarded as a trade secret.

A trade secret is any document, formula, pattern, physical device, idea, process, list, or other information that provides the owner of the information a competitive advantage in the marketplace. Examples of potential trade secrets are provided in Table 5.3.

*Table 5.3. Examples of Potential Trade Secrets*

| | |
|---|---|
| • Business plans | • Marketing plans |
| • Product designs | • Financial forecasts |
| • Customer lists | • Employee rosters |
| • Logs of sales calls | • Laboratory notebooks |
| • E-mail archives | • Notes of staff meetings |
| • Computer files | • Advertising copy (not yet used) |

Unlike patents, copyrights, and trademarks, there is no governmental agency that regulates trade secrets. The Federal Economic Espionage Act, passed in 1996, criminalizes the theft of trade secrets, so designating something as a "trade secret" does have teeth if the secret is adequately protected.

There are two things a new business owner needs to know about trade secrets: What qualifies for trade secret protection and trade secret protection methods.

## What Qualifies for Trade Secret Protection?

Not all information qualifies for trade secret protection. Information that is known to the public or that competitors can discover through legal means (like looking at a company's Web site) doesn't qualify for trade secret protection. If a company passes out brochures at a trade show and which are available to anyone in attendance, nothing in the brochure can typically qualify as a trade secret. Similarly, if a secret is disclosed by mistake it typically loses its trade secret protection. For example, if you inadvertently post your customer list on your Web site and a competitor downloads the list, you're generally out of luck. Simply stated, the general philosophy of trade secret legislation is that the law does not protect a trade secret unless the owner has protected it first.

## Trade Secret Protection Methods

There are two things that a new business can do to protect its trade secrets.

The first is to require all employees, and others on occasion, to sign nondisclosure agreements, as recommended in Chapter 2, Legal Requirements Part 2. Trade secret disputes arise most frequently when an employee leaves a business to join a competitor and is accused of taking confidential information along.

The second method to protect trade secrets is through physical means. The following are examples:

- Restricting access: Many businesses restrict physical access to confidential material to only the employees who have a "need to know."

- Labeling documents: Sensitive documents should be stamped or labeled "confidential" or "proprietary." If possible, these documents should be stored in locked filing cabinets.
- Password protecting confidential computer files. Providing employees with clearance to view confidential information by using secure passwords can restrict information on a company's computer network, Web site, or intranet.
- Maintaining logbooks for access to sensitive information. Many businesses maintain logbooks for sensitive material and make their employees "check in" and "check out" the material.
- Maintaining adequate overall security measures: Commonsense measures are also helpful. You should buy a shredder to destroy documents as appropriate. Desks and files should be locked while not in use if they contain sensitive material. An alarm system should be installed in your facility or office if significant physical or intellectual assets are at risk.

Some of these measures may seem extreme, particularly for a business in the prelaunch stage. Use your judgment in implementing them. Unfortunately, we live in an imperfect world, and you do need to be concerned about securing your confidential information. Steps like shredding documents may seem like overkill at first glance but may be important in ultimately protecting your trade secrets. Believe it or not, there have been cases in which new businesses have caught competitors literally going through the trash bins behind their buildings looking for confidential information.

# APPENDIX

# First 100 Days Plan

**Prelaunch (Days 1–30)**

*Part 5: Protecting Your Intellectual Property*

|  | Requirement | Check when done | Result (fill in below) |
|---|---|---|---|
| Step 1 | Patents | ☐ | Identify the primary product or service that you'll be selling. Explain whether patents apply. If you will be applying for one or more patents, describe the steps you'll go through to make that happen. |
| Step 2 | Copyrights | ☐ | Write a brief policy for your company in regard to copyrights (1–2 paragraphs). Explain the procedure you'll put in place in regard to (a) what materials you'll affix the copyright bug to, (b) what materials you'll apply for copyright protection through the U.S. Copyright Office, and (c) what materials, if any, you'll neither place the copyright bug on nor apply for protection through the U.S. Copyright Office. Make your descriptions specific to your business. |
| Step 3 | Trademarks | ☐ | Write a brief policy for your company in regard to trademarks (1–2 paragraphs). Identify the items on which you'll apply for formal trademark protection. Describe the steps you'll go through to obtain the trademarks. |

*(Continued)*

## Part 5: Protecting Your Intellectual Property (Continued)

|        | Requirement   | Check when done | Result (fill in below) |
|--------|---------------|-----------------|------------------------|
| Step 4 | Trade Secrets | ☐ | Write a brief policy for your company in regard to trade secrets (1–2 paragraphs). Describe how you'll protect your trade secrets, including specific examples based on your particular business. |

# CHAPTER 6

# Establishing a Professional Image

## Introduction

An important topic you should be working on in the prelaunch stage of your business is establishing a professional image. New businesses are at a disadvantage because they are new and it's a risk for potential clients or customers to give them a try. One of the primary ways to reduce the perception of risk is to make a good first impression, and provide people a sense that you're professional and well prepared. In addition, fair or unfair, people will judge you by the material that represents your business. If your logo, stationary, or business cards look shabby or amateurish, people will think you're amateurish too. There isn't a silver bullet for creating a professional image. Instead, it boils down to doing a lot of little things well.

This chapter focuses on a collection of "little things" that, if done well, go a long way in helping a start-up establish a professional image. Part of creating a professional image is building a Web site and establishing a social media presence. These topics will be tackled in Chapter 7, Establishing an Online Presence. This chapter focuses on the items identified as follows. If approached correctly, each of these items can contribute to establishing a professional image for a new business.

| Step 1 | Creating a Logo |
| Step 2 | Selecting a Tagline |
| Step 3 | Business Cards |
| Step 4 | Stationary |
| Step 5 | Signs |
| Step 6 | Phone Systems |
| Step 7 | Little Things That Matter |
| Appendix | First 100 Days Plan: Establishing a Professional Image |

# Step 1: Creating a Logo

A business's logo is the image that represents the company. It can be a graphical image, such as the Nike swoosh logo, one or more words, such as the distinctive way *Coca-Cola* is written, or can be a combination of words and images, like *Walt Disney Pictures* with the image of Sleeping Beauty's Castle in the background. Because the whole idea behind a logo is that it's intended to foster immediate customer recognition, it shouldn't be changed frequently. It should be available prior to a business's launch date, so it can be placed on business cards, stationery, signs, and other items.

You can pursue two paths in designing a logo—trying to design it yourself or hiring someone to design it for you. If you choose the first route, and have an aptitude for design, you may be familiar with graphic design programs that will enable you to design an effective logo. If you're not familiar with graphic design programs, and still want to design it yourself, you can utilize one of the online sites, like LogoYes (http://logoyes.com) or LogoMaker (www.logomaker.com), to help. A fairly simple, yet clean and sharp, logo can be designed on LogoMaker for $49.

If you opt to hire someone to design your logo for you, there are two alternatives. First, you can hire a graphic designer. In most areas, many graphic designers are available, and some will create logos for a very affordable price. The best way to find a graphic designer is to ask other business owners for a referral. Second, there are several online sites that farm-out logo designs to graphic designers, and can get you a choice of several logos. An example is 99designs (http://99designs.com). The way 99designs works is that you post a design request on the site, with details of what you want designed. The listing fee is $39. Over a week or less, designers from all over the world submit design concepts. During the week, you provide feedback and ratings for the submitted designs. At the end of the week you select a winner. The designer is then paid through 99designs. Once the payment is made, all rights to the design you choose are transferred to you. Majority of the designers are freelancers, students, and professional designers working in their spare time to earn extra money. A logo costs between $299 and $699 to have designed on 99designs, depending on the type of contest you run. You can also have brochures, t-shirts, business cards, stationary, signage, Web pages, and similar items designed by 99designs designers in a similar manner.

There is an entire science to logo design, and it's worth your time to do some Internet research, regardless of whether you design your own logo or evaluate the suggested designs of others. A business's logo and its name are the most important symbols of its brand. A well-designed logo depicts the concept and values of the business it represents along with the target market the business has selected. Color, for example, is important. Colors are associated with certain emotions. For instance, loud primary colors, such as red, are meant to attract attention, and are appropriate for products or services that require attention, like a new type of skateboard. Red, white, and blue are used in logos that want to project a patriotic feeling. Green is often associated with the health and hygiene sector. Light blue and silver are often used to highlight diet foods. Subdued tones communicate reliability, quality, and similar traits. Similarly, shapes and font styles fit certain types of businesses. Logos for high-tech businesses are often chiseled and angular, suggesting the business is innovative. In contrast, logos for

Table 6.1. *Tactics That will Help You Design or Select an Appropriate Logo*

| Tactic | Explanation |
|---|---|
| Look at logos of other businesses in your industry. | Do your competitors use firm, conservative images or flashy graphics and fonts? Think about how you want to differentiate your logo from those of your competition. |
| Focus on your message. | Think about what you want to communicate through your logo. Do you want to communicate "lighthearted," like a casual games company might want to communicate, or "serious," like a medical products company might want to communicate? |
| Make it clean, functional, and expandable. | Your logo should be able to grow with your business. It should look as good on a billboard as on a business card. And be sure to create a logo that doesn't wash out in black and white, so it can be faxed and photocopied. |
| Your business name will affect your logo design. | In some cases, your business's name will affect the design of your logo. For example, if you're opening a business called Tropical Drinks, Smoothies and Shakes, your logo may contain a small umbrella sticking out of the sand. |
| Choose a logo that will remain current for an extended period of time. | Don't create a logo that reminds people of a current event. That event will be replaced by other events in the future. Create a logo that isn't tied to a current time period and will remain relevant for an extended period of time. |

*Source*: Adapted from "How to Create a Logo," http://www.entrepreneur.com/article/71902, accessed June 15, 2012.

service-oriented companies are frequently smooth and rounded, hoping to produce the perception that the company is creative and friendly.

Table 6.1 provides additional tactics that will help you design or select an appropriate logo.

## Step 2: Selecting a Tagline

A tagline is a slogan or a catchy phrase that is intended to convey a business's brand in just a few words. A great tagline is also memorable, and helps people quickly understand what your business is about. For example, Zipcar, the car-sharing company, has the tagline "Wheels when you want them." The tagline is right on point in that it reinforces the company's value proposition: If you belong to Zipcar you don't have to own a car, but you can still have a car available to you "when you want" it. Other memorable taglines are Nike: *Just do it* and Maxwell House: *Good to the Last Drop.*

A business's tagline can be used on its literature, advertisements, stationery, business cards, and even invoices. A company has created a successful tagline if the message makes you think of its products or services and the position it has established in the marketplace.

Rules of thumb for creating a tagline include:

- Your tagline should be memorable.
- It should support your business's value proposition to customers.
- It should reflect your business's personality. If your business is a casual dining restaurant, your tagline should have a "casual" tone to it.
- It should be simple. No long words, tongue twisters, or lengthy slogans.
- People should be able to quickly associate it with your business. Once you think you've settled on a tagline, try the following test. Place your business's name in the middle of a list of several businesses' names on the left-hand side of a sheet of paper. Provide a brief description of each business. Then place your tagline on the right-hand side of the paper.

Show the paper to several people who aren't acquainted with your business. See if they can accurately guess to which business the tagline belongs.

## Step 3: Business Cards

Although business cards may seem like a little thing, they're typically given to potential clients, customers, or business partners in the hope that they'll follow-up with you and become a customer or partner. As a result, it's worthwhile to give your business cards some thought and consideration.

The following information should be placed on your business card:

- Your name
- Name of your business or organization
- Address
- Phone number (voice and smartphone)
- E-mail address
- Fax number (if your business sends and receives a lot of faxes)
- Web page address
- Job title
- Tagline or description of the business (if there is enough room and it's appropriate)
- Logo
- Facebook and/or Twitter names if they will be an important part of your online strategy.

This is a long list, so other than your name, the name of your business, and your contact information, you may have to pick and choose some. Similar to a logo and tagline, your business card should convey the overall image of your business. This is a challenge, considering that the standard business card measures two inches by three inches. What a business card should do more than anything else is represent you and your business in a positive manner.

There are many recommendations for how a business card should be designed, including color, wording, and texture. Use common sense. If you'll be opening a financial planning service, you'll want your card to project stability and success, so a white card with black print might be the best choice. In contrast, if you're opening a childcare center and one of your points of differentiation is that your children will be outside a lot engaging in exercise and games, you might want a bright green card that prominently displays your logo, which includes an image of children swinging on a swing.

There are simple rules of thumb for business card design. A business card should be simple and uncluttered. Make sure the typeface is easily readable. Also, make sure that the card shows up well if photographed by a smartphone. A growing number of apps that help people stay organized instruct users to photograph the business cards they receive, and the information on the cards is then stored in easy to retrieve files.

There are deviations from the norm that you can try, as follows. Make sure the deviations remain true to the nature of your business.

- *Nontraditional shapes.* Although they are more expensive, you can get cards in nontraditional shapes. For example, the owner of a new floral shop might have a business card in the shape of a bouquet of flowers. If a nontraditional shape interests you, type "business cards in nontraditional shapes" into the Google search engine and click on images. You'll see hundreds of examples. A downside of choosing a nontraditional shape is that it makes it harder for a man to slip your business card into his billfold or for anyone to slip your card into a pocket designed for business cards in a planner or folder.
- *Textured paper.* Make sure the texture doesn't detract from the card's readability.
- *A larger than normal card.* Business cards can be made larger than normal, and folded over like a mini-brochure.

Once you've selected your business card, you should keep a supply with you at all times. If you go to a conference or trade show, carry enough that you don't run out. Distributing business cards can be your cheapest form of advertising. Some business people attach their business card to all correspondence. It's a judgment call or your part whether this strategy is a good choice for your business.

There are several ways to get business cards printed. Vistaprint (www.vistaprint.com) is an excellent choice. You can essentially design your own card and get 250 cards for $10. You can also have cards designed and printed at office supply stores. The same resource that you tapped to design your logo can often design your business cards and stationary as well.

## Step 4: Stationary

A business's stationary is another one of the "little" thing that contributes to building a professional image. Often, the perception that potential clients and customers form about your business have as much to do with your stationary, business cards, and phone system as your marketing material.

In terms of design, your stationary shouldn't be a standalone accessory. It should include a letterhead that mirrors the font and general appearance of your business cards. It should also include your logo if appropriate. You should select high-quality paper—certainly higher quality than the standard printer paper. If you'll be creating your own stationary by printing it via a word processing program like Microsoft Word, you can buy stationary quality (and weight) paper at office supply stores like Staples and OfficeMax. Some businesses place images on their stationary that are different from their logo. For example, if you're opening a financial planning service, and your business is essentially yourself, you might place a photo of yourself on your stationary. Another example would be placing an image of the building you work in on your stationary. Some businesses use color stationary, such as beige or tan. If you push the limits on color, you should make sure the color you select makes sense. For example, if you're opening a driving range for people to hit golf balls, light green stationary might make sense.

All business stationary should include basic information like the company's name, address, phone number, fax number, e-mail address, and Web site address. You should also include your Facebook and/or Twitter names if you plan to incorporate Facebook and Twitter into your online strategy. Never rely on people to know your return address by referring to the envelope that the letter was mailed in. Once opened, letters often quickly become separated from the envelopes they came in.

Similar to business cards, you can have your stationary designed and printed by an online service like Vistaprint or 99designs, or you can go to an office supply store like Staples or OfficeMax. At the FedEx Store, you can pick out stationary from a catalog of possibilities, and then customize your letterhead. Make sure to order an adequate supply of stationary. Although it might seem like an extravagance to order 250 or 500 sheets of stationary, particularly since so much business is now done online, when you launch your business you don't want to be thinking about reordering stationary. You'll be focused on more important things.

## Step 5: Signs

Businesses vary substantially in terms of the signage they need and use. If you're a professional service business, such as an accounting firm, an engineering firm, a law firm, or a dental practice, you might have a small tasteful sign in front of your building or suite of offices, primarily to help people find you. In contrast, if you're a retailer or restaurant, your sign might your most powerful marketing tool in that it brings in foot and/ or drive by traffic.

Since you probably don't have the knowledge or equipment to make a sign yourself, you'll have to go somewhere. In most communities, there are professional sign makers, like FASTSIGNS, which not only design signs but also install them. There are also online sites, such as eSigns (www.esigns.com), where you can design and order signs. Sign manufacturers vary in terms of how much design help they'll provide you. Many provide substantial help. Make sure you check your local zoning ordinances before you buy a sign. Communities vary considerably in terms of what they allow, as mentioned in earlier chapters. You'll need to get help, either for the sign manufacturer you choose or from a graphic designer with sign experience, to determine how large your sign should be (within the parameters of what's permissible in your area). A wealth of practical information about signs and the different things you should be thinking about when designing a sign for your business is available through the United States Sign Council at www.ussc.org.

The same companies that manufacture signs also manufacture banners, yard signs, and car and truck magnets (which are removable signs that can be placed on the sides of cars and trucks). Some service business, such as carpet cleaning business, painters, and plumbers, report that their number one source of new customers is people who see their trucks in front of people's homes and stop and write down the phone number on the side of the truck. This anecdote illustrates the value of signs in some contexts.

Table 6.2 contains additional tips for designing and installing effective signs.

**Table 6.2. Tips for Effective Signs**

| Tip | Explanation |
|-----|-------------|
| Less is more. | Don't design a sign that's cluttered. |
| First impressions count. | Your sign might be the first thing people see regarding your business, so it's your opportunity to make a favorable first impression. Don't skimp on the quality of the sign you buy, particularly if you'll be relying on it to bring in business. |
| Capture people's attention. | There should be something about your sign that captures people's attention. It might be a bold color, attractive scenery, or contrasting colors. Once you get your target audience's attention, you can then provide them your message. |
| Make sure your sign is visible all year long. | Have you ever seen a sign that's partly blocked by a tree branch or shrub? Try to avoid this type of distraction. |
| Consider lighting your sign at night. | Consider lighting your sign at night if it's allowable under your area's zoning restrictions. |
| Use your sign to set the mood. | Signs can often set the mood for a business. Your sign would look much different if you're a day spa opposed to a pet store. |
| Think carefully about where your sign is visible from. | Make sure your sign is clearly visible from the point where most people will be looking at it. For instance, if your business is located along a city street, make sure your sign is visible for approaching cars, not just cars directly in front of your building. Drivers will be more apt to notice your sign as they approach your business, not when they're passing by. |
| Be careful in choosing background colors. | When choosing a background color for your sign, make sure you don't use something that will make it difficult to focus on the main message. |

# Step 6: Phone System

Most new businesses buy a phone system of some kind. The five most popular types of phone systems are shown in Table 6.3. Each one of these systems can be set up in a manner that allows a new business to make and answer calls in a professional manner.

*Table 6.3.  Five Most Popular Types of Phone Systems*

| Type of system | Description |
|---|---|
| Keyless System (KSU-less) | Suitable for businesses with less than 10 employees. The systems support two to four phone lines and offer only the most basic features. The phones do not require a key system unit (KSU) or central control unit because the technology is built right into the phones. The system doesn't grow well with a business, but the phones are easy to move if you relocate your business. This is the type of system where any user can make an outgoing call simply by pressing one of the outside line buttons to get a line (the line then lights up to show that it's in use). Any user can pick up an incoming call by simply pressing a button that is flashing. |
| Key Systems (KSU) | Suitable for businesses with 10 to 40 employees. System offers the most basic telephone needs for a company, yet it can be upgraded as your business grows. It offers multiple lines and is support by a KSU. Key Systems in general are improving, and many now offer some of the benefits of a PBX. |
| Private Branch Exchange Systems (PBX) | Suitable for businesses with 50+ employees. This is the type of system used by large businesses. It has the most advanced features. It requires installation from a telecom vendor and is the most expensive of the four choices. This is the type of unit that needs a cabinet of electronics to direct incoming calls. It's the type of system where you press 9 to get an outgoing line. |
| Voice Over Internet Protocol System (VoIP) | Suitable for any size company. The system directs a call through the Internet rather than traditional phone lines. VoIP systems are gaining popularity among all sizes of businesses. |
| All Cellular System | Suitable for very small businesses, particularly one-person firms. |

*Source:* Adapted from DiSilvestro, A. (2012, February 28). StartupNation Web site (www.startupnation). Accessed June 17, 2012.

The choice you make will hinge largely on the type of business you're starting. For example, if you're opening a retail store, a service business that anticipates a lot of incoming calls, or will be setting up an office where several people will work, a traditional landline key system still makes sense. VoIP is also an option, but you should check around to see if other businesses are having good luck with VoIP systems in your area. VoIP relies on power being constantly on, so it might not be a good choice in areas where intermittent power outages are common. Landlines are also very stable, and tend to have good voice quality. However, if you're starting a business where you will be on the road a lot, will meet with clients primarily out of your office, or you're a one-person firm, utilizing a VoIP service or going strictly cellular may make perfect sense.

There are a number of enhancements to phone services that small business can utilize to not only appear professional, but also to enhance their ability to communicate. Services like Google Voice can be configured around your business land line, so that any call that rings on your business phone can also ring on your home phone or smartphone, and you can listen to voice mail wherever you are, and forward it to your e-mail account.

There are also a growing number of services that provide small businesses access to 800 numbers for as little as $10 a month. The advantage of having an 800 number is that it allows a business to promote one number, and the caller can be routed to the appropriate person, no matter where the employee is. An 800 number can also be set up in multiple ways. It can be set up so that when a caller calls in, the system will say Press 1 for John Smith, Press 2 for Julie Williams, Press 3 for Sam Jenkins, and so forth. Or it can be set up to say Press 1 to Place an Order, Press 2 for Customer Service, Press 3 for Returns, Press 4 to Reach an Operator, or whatever you want. An 800 number can be set up this way even if you're launching a single-person firm. Even though the system says Press 1 to Place an Order, Press 2 for Customer Service, and so on, all calls would be directed to you. Some start-ups like this because it makes their business appear to be bigger than it is. For an additional fee, you can obtain a vanity 800 number (like 1-800-FLOWERS) if the number is available. For example, the fictitious company Constant Comfort Air Handler introduced in the previous chapter might try to get the number 1-800-COMFORTAIR. RingCental (www.ringcentral.com) and Grasshopper (www.grasshopper .com) are examples of companies that specialize in providing 800 numbers to small businesses.

## Step 7: Little Things That Matter

There are also a number of little things regarding establishing a professional image to consider.

### Having a Business e-mail Address

It's important to have a business e-mail address. If you launch a business, like Constant Comfort Air Handler, and your business card says your e-mail address is Steve.Jones @gmail.com, it makes your company appear amateurish. It would be much better to have an e-mail address that says Steve.Jones @constantcomfortairhandler.com. You can easily set up e-mail addresses like this once you purchase an Internet domain name (more about domain names in Chapter 7, Establishing an Online Presence). Having an e-mail address that's tied to your businesses name makes you look much more professional.

### Dress

You should consider the norms of your industry and how your business plans to differentiate itself in choosing how you and your employees dress while at work. If you're an Internet company whose public face is your Web site, and your customers never actually see you or your employees, dress may not matter. In fact, you may have better luck attracting talented employees if you allow them to dress informally. In contrast, if you're starting a lawn care service and you plan to differentiate your business by providing a highly reliable, consistent, and professional service to your customers, you might want your employees to wear polo shirts with your company name on them, tan slacks or shorts, and ball caps with your company logo. You could then tell prospective clients, "Not only will we show up on time and give you consistent, reliable, and professional service, you'll immediately recognize our employees by their green polo shirts, tan slacks or shorts, and ball cap with our logo." In this scenario your employees' dress reinforces what differentiates you from your competitors—consistency and professionalism.

Polo shirts with your business's name on them are a good choice under a number of circumstances. Anytime you wear a shirt or a cap with your company's name or logo on it you're essentially "wearing your brand." It's a particularly good approach for service employees who will be going to customer's homes or businesses. It's also a good way to dress at trade shows.

### List Your Business in Directories

Don't forget to list your business in directories. Rather than checking the yellow pages to find a graphic designer or plumber, people are increasingly turning to the Internet. For example, if someone in Sioux Falls, South Dakota is looking for a graphic designer, their first step will likely be to type "graphic designers in Sioux Falls" into the Google search engine and see what happens.

Many directories allow businesses to sign up for free, but you have to sign up. You typically don't get listed automatically. You can list your business in a number of online directories fairly quickly. Table 6.4 contains a sample of Web sites that maintain directories, which help people find you on the Internet. The URL for the place to sign-up is also included.

**Table 6.4. Sample of Directories that Help People Find You on the Internet (Includes Both Free and Fee-Based Services)**

| | |
|---|---|
| Google | http://accounts.google.com |
| Bing | www.bing.com/local |
| Yahoo! | http://listings.local.yahoo.com/ |
| Merchant Circle | http://www.merchantcircle.com/signup/ |
| YellowPages.com | www.yellowpages.com |
| Whitepages | http://www.whitepages.com/ |
| Yellowbook | www.yellowbook.com |
| Local.com | https://advertise.local.com/ |
| LinkedIn | http://www.linkedin.com/ |
| Supermedia | https://www.supermedia.com/business-listings |
| Mapquest | http://help.mapquest.com/topic/mapquest-local-business-center/ |

## *Be Easy to Reach*

Nothing annoys potential customers more than not being able to reach you. As a result, set up several ways for customers to reach you. Consider placing on every page of your Web site your telephone number, e-mail address, and social media information (to the extent you're using social media), such as your Twitter, Facebook, and LinkedIn contact information. If you'd like to see an example of this, go to Zappos.com. The company's 800 number is on every page of its Web site.

You can also achieve a similar objective by placing your contact information on your marketing brochures, stationary, invoices, and other information that you distribute to prospects and customers. If you don't want to give out your personal e-mail address, you can set up an e-mail address such as info@constantcomfortairhandler.com. If you don't want to give out your personal or business telephone number, you can ask customers to contact any other number you're using (including an 800 number) and have the calls forwarded to your number.

# APPENDIX

# First 100 Days Plan

## Prelaunch (Days 1–30)

### Part 6: Establishing a Professional Image

| | Requirement | Check when done | Result (fill in below) |
|---|---|---|---|
| Step 1 | Creating a logo | ☐ | Design a logo for your company. You can design the logo in PowerPoint, a drawing program you're familiar with, via one of the online services that help people design logos, or on a piece of paper. Briefly describe the philosophy behind your logo. |
| Step 2 | Selecting a tagline | ☐ | Write a tagline for your business. It shouldn't be more than a few words long. |
| Step 3 | Business cards | ☐ | Design a business card for your company. |
| Step 4 | Stationary | ☐ | Describe what your stationary and return envelopes will look like. |

| | Requirement | Check when done | Result (fill in below) |
|---|---|---|---|
| Step 5 | Signs | ☐ | Describe the signs you'll need, what they'll look like, and whether there are sign ordinances in your area that you'll need to comply with. |
| Step 6 | Phone systems | ☐ | Select the phone system you'd start out with, and explain the rationale for your selection. |
| Step 7 | Little things that matter | ☐ | Describe three little things that matter in terms of establishing a professional image (and will be particularly important for your start-up) not mentioned in the chapter. |

# CHAPTER 7

# Establishing an Online Presence

## Introduction

Regardless of the type of business you're starting, having an online presence is a necessity. Think about what the average person will do when they hear about your business. Often, the first thing they do is look for your Web site. If you don't have one or the one you have is poorly done, the prospect may not take you seriously.

You'll need to establish on online presence in other areas. One of the most powerful ways is to build an e-mail list of prospects and customers who opt for a weekly or monthly newsletter that provides them interesting information and subtly promotes your products. A start-up should also have a social media strategy. The strategy may call for extensive use of social media, moderate use, or no use at all. It would be rare for a start-up to have no social media presence, but it is an area that requires careful thought. The portion of this chapter devoted to social media will provide criteria for determining the social media strategy that's appropriate for your business, and the social media sites that are available to participate in. Finally, for those start-ups that plan to sell online, there are certain steps that should be taken in the prelaunch stage of The First 100 Days Plan to gear up for online commerce.

The following are the steps in The First 100 Days Plan covered in this chapter:

| Step 1 | Creating a Web Site |
|---|---|
| Step 2 | Building an e-mail List |
| Step 3 | Establishing a Social Media Strategy |
| Step 4 | Preparing to Sell Online if Applicable |
| Appendix | First 100 Days Plan: Establishing an Online Presence |

## Step 1: Creating a Web Site

Although building a Web site takes money and effort, it's a business necessity. Creating a Web site involves five key steps: obtaining an Internet domain name, determining the objectives of your Web Site, building your Web Site, the appearance and design of your Web site, and monitoring the site to access and improve its effectiveness.

### *Obtaining an Internet Domain Name*

Your first task is to obtain an Internet domain name. A domain name is a business's Internet address (i.e., www.apple.com). Most business's want their domain name to be the same name as their business's name. It's easy to register an Internet domain name through an online registration service such as GoDaddy (www.godaddy.com) or Network Solutions (www.networksolutions.com). The standard fee for registering and maintaining a domain name is about $12 per year. Once you've registered a domain name, you can keep it indefinitely as long as you pay the yearly fee.

In most cases, the exact name you're looking for won't be available. That's because the most obvious names have been taken. You can usually work around that complication by using a little imagination. For example, say you're starting a business named Jones Engineering and find that the Internet domain name www.jonesengineering.com is already taken. You can often tweak the name and preserve its intent. For example, as of the time of this writing (June 2012), the domain name www.jones engineeringinc.com was available. If Jones Engineering was incorporated, that might be a perfectly acceptable domain name. Try to avoid obtaining a domain name other than a .com name. A permutation of the name you really want, like jonesengineeringinc rather than jonesengineering, is typically a better choice than trying to use a .org or a .net name as your primary domain name.

After you obtain your Internet domain name, you'll have to engage a hosting service to host your Web site. Most of the domain name registration services offer hosting services, and there would be local hosting services in your area, including your Internet access provider. The best way to find a reliable hosting service is to ask other businesspeople in your area who they use.

### Determining the Objectives of Your Web Site

There are many options regarding the look and functionality of a Web site, so it's important to determine what you want your Web site to accomplish before you start building it. The most important questions to ask are who will be coming to your Web site and what will they be looking for when they get there? There are basically three levels of Web sites to choose from, as shown in Table 7.1.

**Table 7.1. Three Levels of Web Sites to Choose From**

| | |
|---|---|
| Basic Web Site | A basic Web Site introduces your business and consists of a few pages that highlight your product or service, archive news releases and press about your business, and provide contact information. These sites are usually created from a template and costs as little as $200 if you build it yourself or between $1,000 and $3,000 if you hire someone else to do it. |
| Intermediate Web Site | An intermediate Web Site allows you to receive online requests, sell products via a shopping cart, process credit cards, and display more information than a basic site. These sites are customized by a Web site designer and cost between $5,000 and $15,000. |
| Advanced Web Site | An advanced site does everything an intermediate site does along with complex tasks such as tracking inventory and maintaining customer databases. These sites involve specialized programming and run $5,000 and up. |

Regardless of the type of site you choose, you shouldn't put it up until its ready. Consumers react negatively to sites that are only partially functional or say "Under Construction." You should put your Web site address on all your promotional and correspondence material. This material includes your brochures, advertisements, business cards, and stationary.

### Building Your Web Site

If you're content with a basic Web site and have a limited budget, there are do-it-yourself Web site packages available through vendors such as

Squarespace (www.squarespace.com) and Weebly (www.weebly.com). These companies sell packages that include instructions and tools for building a Web site, along with the services necessary to launch and maintain the site. If you don't want to do the work yourself, or you want an intermediate or advanced site, you'll have to hire a Web design firm or a freelancer who's capable of building Web sites. Good sites for locating freelances include Guru (www.guru.com) and Elance (www.elance.com). Avoid turning over the entire design and maintenance of your Web site to someone else. Although you may need a Web design firm to build and host your site, you should learn how to add content to your site and make changes on your own.

Regardless of whether you build your own site or someone does it for you, you should make sure to focus attention on techniques that can be utilized to push your Web site as close to the top of the Google search results as possible. This is a practice referred to as search engine optimization (SEO). The specific tactics involved with SEO are beyond the scope of this book, but is something you can learn about via Internet research or by consulting a Web design firm or search engine optimization expert. There are also many good books and Web sites that focus on SEO. Once a site is built, you must also maintain it. For example, if your site contains links to other sites, you should periodically check the links to make sure the sites you're linking to are still active. If your site archives your press releases, you should post new press releases as soon as they're released to the news media.

### The Appearance and Design of Your Web Site

The physical appearance of your Web site should project your company's image and brand. Its color scheme and overall look should tie in with your other promotional material, including your logo, your business cards, your signs, and so forth.

There are many excellent resources that focus on Web Site design. Table 7.2 contains a list of questions you should ask when building your site and on a periodic basis after it's up and running.

*Table 7.2. Questions You Should Ask When Building Your Web Site and on a Periodic Basis Once It's Up and Running*

| | |
|---|---|
| Is it visually appealing? | Do the pages load quickly? |
| Is the layout well organized? | Is the site easy to navigate? |
| Is the content meaningful? | Is the site easy to find? |
| Does the site answer the most obvious questions that someone coming to the site might have? | Does the site emphasize the points that differentiate my company from my competitors? |
| If a potential customer or client wants to place an order, is that possible? | Is there a "contact us" link or page that provides visitors instructions for how to contact you? |
| Is it easy for visitors to sign-up for your e-mail newsletter or blog? (if you have one or both) | Does every page on the site look like it belongs to the same site? |

If you want to see how not to design a Web site, go to www.websites thatsuck.com. The site provides good information on the do's and don'ts of Web site design.

### Monitoring Your Web Site to Assess and Improve Its Effectiveness

The final step in launching and maintaining a Web Site is to monitor its effectiveness and make changes when necessary. You can test the usability of your site by asking people to navigate the site while you watch, and take note of when they seem to be confused or have trouble finding the information they need. There are also Web-based services that will conduct more sophisticated usability tests for a fee. For example, UserTesting (www.usertesting.com) will provide you a video of users speaking their thoughts as they navigate your site for $39 per user. Similarly, Open-Hallway (www.openhallway.com) offers tired pricing (starting at $49 per month) that provides ongoing usability testing of your Web site.

You should also investigate the field of web analytics. When you launch your site, you must hire a company to host it. Make sure that your host is set up to provide you statistics on the usage of your site, or hire a separate company to give you the information. You can also use Google Analytics (www.google.com/analytics), which is a free service. A sample of the information you can obtain, which is what web analytics refers to, is as follows:

- The number of visitors you have each hour, day, and week of the month.
- The number of unique visitors that you receive (on a daily or weekly basis).
- A report on where your visitors come from.
- Insights into how visitors use your site.
- A report on what are most frequently viewed pages on your Web site and how long do people stay on your Web Site.
- What search terms are visitors using to find your site?
- What other Web sites link to your site.

By analyzing this type of information, you can see the pages and products that people are most interested in, whether there are more number of people visiting a particular product page but not buying (indicating the page needs to be reworded), and how well offline promotional campaigns are working. For example, once you're up and running, you might run ads in a local newspaper promoting your business. If you prominently display your Web site address in your ads, you could in part measure the success of the newspaper ad campaign by monitoring the degree to which the ads increased traffic to your Web Site.

## Step 2: Building an e-mail List

You should consider putting mechanisms in place to capture your prospects' and customers' e-mail addresses for the purposes of distributing a monthly or quarterly newsletter and for future e-mail marketing. Despite the promise of social media, e-mail is still a powerful tool to keep in touch with customers and strengthen your relationship with them. When you ask your prospects or customers for their e-mail address, you should ask them to "opt-in" to receiving e-mail messages from you. If you don't do this, you'll be essentially spamming your customers, which you don't want to do.

It's important that you put the mechanisms in place to start building your e-mail list right away, so you (and your employees if you have employees) start making it a part of your daily routine. In the postlaunch

ESTABLISHING AN ONLINE PRESENCE    119

phase of the First 100 Days Plan, recommendations will be provided for how to use the list. If you build a robust e-mail list, it can become a key component of your overall marketing strategy.

Table 7.3 provides suggestions for how to capture your prospects and customer's e-mail addresses.

**Table 7.3. How to Build an e-mail List**

| Method for capturing e-mail addresses | Explanation |
|---|---|
| Create a sign-up page on your Web site. | A link to a sign-up page should be placed on the front page of your Web site, allowing visitors to provide you their e-mail address and to opt-in to subscribing to your newsletter and other material. |
| Ask customers to opt-in at the time of purchase. | Whether you're selling online or in a bricks-and-mortar format, you should ask customers for their e-mail address and for permission to send them your newsletter and other material. |
| Run contests, giveaways, or offer coupons. | You can run a contest, offer a giveaway, or offer coupons to people who provide you their e-mail address. If you do this, you should disclose to the people who are signing up that they'll start receiving your e-mail newsletter and other e-mail correspondence from you. |
| Place people on the list who are in your network and you think might benefit from being on your list. | Look through your business cards, contacts, and think of the people you know who may be good prospects for your business, and ask permission to place them on your e-mail list. Disclose that, by being on the list, they'll receive e-mail messages from you periodically. |
| Ask for e-mail addresses from people who contact you by phone. | If appropriate, ask people who contact you by phone for their e-mail address, and ask permission to send them your newsletter and other material. |
| Trade shows. | Trade shows are an ideal venue to collect e-mail addresses. Figure out how to give people who stop by your booth an easy way to sign up for more information via your newsletter or other material. |
| Social media. | Businesses are increasingly using social media to build their e-mail lists. For example, you could place a form on your Facebook page asking people to provide you their e-mail address to sign up for your newsletter and other material. |
| Allow people who receive your newsletter to forward it to others. | Provide a mechanism for people who receive your newsletter to forward it to other people and businesses that they think could benefit from it, and have a way for those people to provide you their e-mail address to start subscribing to your material. |

## Step 3: Establish a Social Media Strategy

Social media consists primarily of blogging and establishing a presence and connecting with customers and others through social networking sites, such as Facebook, Twitter, Google+, and Pinterest. Social media can help a business grow its influence, drive traffic to its Web site, provide service to its customers, and generate sales leads. Although utilizing social media is appropriate in many contexts, you shouldn't do it just because it's the popular thing to do. Thinking through the social media strategy that's right for your start-up and then getting it up and running involves two key topics: Determining the social media strategy that's appropriate for your business and selecting the social media sites to participate in.

### Determining the Social Media Strategy That's Appropriate for Your Business

There are three criteria that are commonly used to help business's discern whether using social media is a good choice for them.

Criterion 1: Are your prospects and customers active users of social media?

The first question to ask is whether the people in your target market are active social media users, and whether they'd be open to be engaged by you via social media sites such as Facebook and Twitter. You can get an indication of this by determining whether your competitors are using social media, and whether their social media campaigns appear to be vibrant. There are also services that maintain demographic profiles of those who use specific social networks, broken down by gender, age, income, educational level, and other categories. This information may be helpful for you to determine how active people are in your target market. Table 7.4 includes data from KISSMetrics (http://blog.kissmetrics.com), a company that collects this type of information, as of June 2012. Looking at the data, it's clear that if you're target market is primarily male, earns $150,00 a year or more, is 55 years and older, and has a Bachelor's Degree or Graduate Degree, social media may not be a good choice for you. In contrast, if your target audience is both male and female, earns between $25,000 and $75,000 a year, and is 18–44 years old, your target market is very active in social media. That doesn't mean you should rush into using social media,

*Table 7.4. Who Uses Facebook and Twitter?*

| Criteria | Facebook | Twitter |
|---|---|---|
| Gender | Male—46%<br>Female—54% | Male—48%<br>Female—52% |
| Income | $5K – $25K—12%<br>$25K – $50K—34%<br>$50K – 75K—32%<br>75K—100K—12%<br>100K—150K—7%<br>150K+—4% | $5K – $25K—15%<br>$25K – $50K—33%<br>$50K – 75K—25%<br>75K—100K—16%<br>100K—150K—7%<br>150K+—4% |
| Age | 0–18—7%<br>18–24—11%<br>25–34—24%<br>35–44—22%<br>45–54—26%<br>55–64—9%<br>65+—2% | 0–18—4%<br>18–24—11%<br>25–34—27%<br>35–44—30%<br>45–54—18%<br>55–64—8%<br>65+—2% |
| Educational Level | No HS Diploma—10%<br>High School—10%<br>Some College—55%<br>Bachelor's Degree—18%<br>Graduate Degree—8% | No HS Diploma—7%<br>High School—7%<br>Some College—49%<br>Bachelor's Degree—28%<br>Graduate Degree—9% |

*Source*: Division of Social Network Users by Age, KISSMetrics (http://blog.kissmetrics.com/social-media-by-demographic), Accessed June 20, 2012.

but it does give you an indication of the social media demographics of your target market.

Criterion 2: Do you have the resources and time to invest in social media?

There is always the issue of resources. Although social media platforms such as Facebook, Twitter, and Pinterest are free, your time is not. Every hour you spend on social media is an hour you're not spending on another business-related activity. In addition, once you set up a Facebook page or Twitter account it must be continually updated to remain relevant. A Facebook page or Twitter account that looks like it's been neglected is worse than having no account at all.

Criterion 3: Are there more effective ways than social media to connect with your customers and to market to them?

This is a judgment call you'll have to make, not only in regard to whether to initiate a social media strategy now, but also throughout the life of your business. Although social media is an effective medium in many contexts, traditional media still has appeal.

### Selecting the Social Media Sites to Participate In

There are several distinct social media platforms. The first is blogs. The idea behind blogs is that they familiarize people with a business and help build an emotional bond between a business and its customers. The key to maintaining a successful blog is to keep it fresh and make it informative and fun. It should also engage its readers in the "industry" and "lifestyle" that a company promotes as much as a company's products or services. It should also include material and activities that cause readers to continually come back. For example, if you're opening a women's clothing store, you might ask the people who visit your blog to post photos of themselves wearing a garment that they bought at your store, and then award a cash prize for the person who bought an article of clothing that "best matches the color of their eyes," or something fun like that. You might also post photos of "behind the scenes" glimpses of what it's like to work at your store or business. For example, if you bring your dog to work each day, you might post photos of your dog hanging out at the back of your store. Or, if you're managing a Web site, you might post photos of your dog sleeping under your desk or barking at your fax machine. Blog entries like this actually cause people to more emotionally bond with your business. One thing you don't want to do with a blog or any social media platform is to use it as a megaphone for constantly promoting your products. People will quickly tire of that strategy and move on to more engaging activities.

Social networks such as Facebook, Twitter, and Google+ also have benefits. Facebook's numbers are huge, which make it particularly attractive. As of May 2012, Facebook had over 900 million users. The company has also made itself more attractive to businesses since launching a family of social plugins in April 2010. Social plugins are tools that Web sites can use to provide its users with personalized and social experiences. Facebook's most popular social plugins, which can be installed on your Web site, include the Like button, the Send button, and the Comment box. These social plugins allow people to share their experiences off Facebook with their friends on Facebook. The Send button, for example, lets users share pages from a company's Web site on their Facebook page with one click. As a result, if a young woman bought a pair of shoes from an online shoe site, and the site was equipped with the Facebook Send plugin, she could immediately post a picture and description of the shoes on her Facebook page and write a comment about the purchase. She might say, "Hey everyone, look at the cool shoes I just bought at _____ (name of store)." This is tantamount to free advertising for the online store.

Businesses also establish a presence on Facebook and Twitter to build a community around their products and services. The benefits include brand building, engaging customers, and getting lead generation. Coupons and special promotional offers can also be posted or described. For example, savvy shoppers often check the Web sites, blogs, Facebook pages, and Twitter accounts of the companies from which they plan to buy a major item before they make the purchase to see if there are any coupons or special promotions being offered. Sometimes you don't even need to print the coupon; you can simply take your smartphone to the store and have them scan the coupon from your phone. In regard to engaging customers, companies often use platforms such as Twitter to post both fun and informative material that's of particular interest to their clientele. For example, if you're running a daycare center, you might post updates throughout the day, talking about what the kids are doing, and post an occasional cute photo. Imagine how that might engage parents who have kids at the center. In addition, you might periodically post material that pertains to child safety, nutritional issues for children, recommendations for good books and videos for kids, and so forth. These types of posts help you engage customers without seeming self-serving. You could also focus on lead generation. For example, a childcare center might post on its Facebook page the application form for parents who don't currently have a child enrolled in their center but are interesting in applying.

There are a growing number of additional social media outlets from which firms can benefit. For example, many businesses post videos on YouTube. YouTube now allows heavy users the ability to create a YouTube channel to archive its videos and create its own YouTube site. Businesses can also establish a presence on niche social networking sites that are consistent with the mission and product offerings. An example is Care 2 (www.care2.com), which is an online community that promotes a healthy and green lifestyle and takes action on social causes.

## Step 4: Preparing to Sell Online if Applicable

If you've decided that you'll be selling products online, there are several steps that you need to take to prepare your business for that. The company or freelancer who builds your Web site can help you with tasks, but it's still your responsibility to make sure that steps are completed and that you have a sufficient infrastructure to support online sales.

Table 7.5 provides a list of the steps that must be taken to prepare for and eventually initiate online sales. These steps focus on the "backend" of online sales.

*Table 7.5. Steps That Must be Taken to Prepare for and Initiate Online Sales*

| Step | Explanation |
|------|-------------|
| Make sure your online transactions are secure | You'll need to make sure that your online transactions are secure. SSL (secure socket layer) encryption protects your customer's confidential information, including their credit card number and personal information, during a transaction. This functionality can be provided by your Web hosting company, or you can secure it on your own. |
| Install a shopping cart | You'll need to install a shopping cart on your Web site. They are many to choose from. |
| Online payments | You'll need a way to accept online payments. You can arrange a Merchant account through a bank, which allows you to accept credit cards and debit cards, or pursue alternative options, such as PayPal. |
| Privacy policy | You'll need to write a privacy policy for your Web site that will protect your business and provide your customers with trust in your site. |
| Order fulfillment | You'll need to have a clearly worked out order fulfillment system. Quick turnaround time is critical in providing high levels of customer service. |
| Constant updates | You'll need to constantly update your site with new content and merchandise to keep customers coming back. |
| Contact us | As with any Web site, you should provide a way for customers to contact you if they're experiencing problems with your site or have a question about an order. |

# APPENDIX

# First 100 Days Plan

## Prelaunch (Days 1–30)

### *Part 7: Establishing an Online Presence*

|         | Requirement | Check when done | Result (fill in below) |
|---------|-------------|-----------------|------------------------|
| Step 1  | Creating a Web site | ☐ | Report your Internet domain name. You don't have to buy the name, but it must be a name that's available. It can also be a name you already own or just purchased. |
|         |             |   | Of the three levels of Web site, describe the level of site that you think is appropriate for your business. |
|         |             |   | Describe the objectives of your site. |
|         |             |   | Describe whether you'd build your site yourself or if you'd hire someone to do it. Speculate on who you would hire. |
|         |             |   | On a piece of paper, draw the front page of your business's Web site. |
|         |             |   | Describe the most important analytics that you'd collect for your site. |
| Step 2  | Building an e-mail list | ☐ | Describe how you'd build an e-mail list for your business. |

| | Requirement | Check when done | Result (fill in below) |
|---|---|---|---|
| Step 3 | Establishing a social media strategy | ☐ | Describe whether your use of social media will be (a) extensive, (b) moderate, or (c) you'll have no social media strategy at all. Describe the rationale for your decision.<br><br>Describe, in sufficient detail, what the social media strategy for your business will be. Include a description of the social media site you'll participate in, and your objectives for participating in each site. |
| Step 4 | Preparing to sell online if applicable | ☐ | Report whether you plan to sell online. If you do, describe the steps you'll take to prepare to sell online. You may expand on the steps listed in Chapter 7. |

# SECTION 2

# Postlaunch Days 31–100

# CHAPTER 8

# Creating a Sales Process and Your First Sale

## Introduction

This chapter transitions the First 100 Days Plan from the prelaunch phases (Chapters 1–7) to postlaunch phase (Chapters 8–14). As mentioned in the introduction, for most businesses there isn't a clear "launch" date. That doesn't need to be the case for your business. Now that you have the steps in place covered in Chapters 1–7, you should be prepared to open your doors and start selling your product or service.

The first thing to do is focus on sales. Ultimately, nothing matters in your business unless you're able to sell your product or service. The following steps allow you to approach selling in a purposeful, systematic manner. A critical milestone is making your first sale. But you don't want that to happen by happenstance. You want your first sale, and all subsequent sales, to result from a systematic, repeatable process that will enable you to sustain and grow your business.

It's also important to know as much as possible about your customers. How you structure your sales process will hinge on the manner in which your customers buy. Study your initial prospects and customers carefully, and as you gain insight into what causes them to buy or not buy from you, adjust your sales process (and in some cases tweak your product or service) accordingly. Once you launch your business, you should also find a systematic way to record insights about what is working and what isn't. In the prelaunch stage of a business, a business is a set of hypotheses waiting to be tested. Once you launch, you start testing the hypotheses, and you should record the results of the tests.

The following are the steps in The First 100 Days Plan covered in this chapter:

| | |
|---|---|
| Step 1 | Creating a Sales Process. |
| Step 2 | Implementing the Sales Process. |
| Step 3 | Understanding Your Customer's Buying Cycle |
| Step 4 | Making Your First Sale. |
| Step 5 | Measuring Results and Reviewing the Sales Process for Improvements. |
| Appendix | First 100 Days Plan: Creating a Sales Process and Your First Sale |

## Step 1: Creating a Sales Process

A business's sales process depicts the steps it goes through to identify prospects and close sales. It doesn't matter whether a business is selling directly to customers or through an intermediary such as a distributor or wholesaler; it still has a process through which it makes sales.

Some companies simply wing it when it comes to sales, which isn't recommended. It's much better to have a well-thought-out approach to prospect customers and closing sales. A formal sales process involves a number of identifiable steps. Although the process varies by firm (and industry), it generally includes seven steps, as shown in Table 8.1. It's very helpful to actually map out the process, so you and your salespeople can visually see the progression of steps that are needed to close sales.

*Table 8.1. Sales Process*

| | |
|---|---|
| Step 1 | Prospect for (or gather) sales leads |
| Step 2 | Make the initial contact |
| Step 3 | Qualify the lead |
| Step 4 | Make the sales presentation |
| Step 5 | Meet objections and concerns |
| Step 6 | Close the sale |
| Step 7 | Follow-up |

Following a formal or structured process to generate and close sales benefits a business in five ways. First, it enables a business to fine-tune its approach to sales and build uniformity into the process. Second, if it's clear, selling becomes a set of steps, rather than an awkward process where you're always unsure about what to do next. Third, the process helps qualify leads. One of the most frustrating things you'll encounter selling is to spend time and effort working with a potential buyer, only to find out that the buyer doesn't have the money or authority to make a purchase. Fourth, by breaking the sales process into steps, if you find that one part of the process is particularly difficult (like meeting objections), you can isolate that part of the process and make improvements. Finally, a fine-tuned sales process helps your company scale up or grow. By having a repeatable process that works, you can teach it to new salespeople who can become productive quickly and help ramp up your overall sales.

If you're not convinced that businesses actually use a sales process, or if you'd like to see the sales process in action, try this experiment (take a copy of the sales process with you to secretly refer to). Go to a car dealership in your area. When you get there, stop and pause and ask yourself why you picked that dealership. If it's not the closest to where you work or live, it's probably because they have been reaching out to you, even if it's through ads (Step 1: Prospecting). If the dealership is sharp, you'll be approached by a salesperson who immediately tries to build rapport (Step 2: Initial contact). Act like you don't know what kind of car you want to look at, and the salesperson will ask you your price range, ask you where you work (which helps them guess how much money you make), ask about what you plan to use the car for, and so forth (Step 3: Qualifying the lead). The salesperson will then show you a car and start telling you about it (Step 4: Sales presentation). Start expressing objections and concerns (the price is too high, it doesn't have a sunroof, wrong color), and the salesperson will have readymade answers to each objection (Step 5: Meeting objections and concerns). Then hesitate some, and the salesperson will say something like, "I'd like to get you in this car today. Let me talk to my sales manager to see if we can bend a little on the price, to make you feel better. If we come down $1,500 on the price, can I write it up for you? (Step 6: Closing the Sales). If you actually bought the car, you'd get a call from the salesperson a week or so later and he or she would say "How's that new car!" (Step 7: Follow-up). Some businesses will tack on one additional step to the sales process, which is trying to obtain follow-up sales. If this is the case in the dealership you visited, if you bought the car and the salesperson called you a week or so later, he or she would start by saying "How's that new car!" and after you chatted a few minutes would say something like, "We talked about the extended warranty when you bought the car. I could tell you're interested—it's a great way to protect your investment. It's not too late. We can get you the extended warranty for up to 30 days after the sale. I'll be in at 6:00 pm tomorrow night. Any chance you could stop by?"

While this process sounds canned, it's worked in the auto sales industry for decades.

## Step 2: Implementing the Sales Process

The best way to implement the sales process is to list the seven steps in the process, and then write procedures for how each step should be executed. You should do this even if you're a one-person business. An example of a sales process, which is better fleshed out than the preceding car dealership example, is provided in Table 8.2. It's for a fictitious company named Prime Adult Fitness, and includes action steps for each step in the process. The example comes from the book *Preparing Effective Business Plans* by Bruce R. Barringer (the author of this book). Prime Adult Fitness is a fitness center for people 50 years old or older. Its mission is to make exercise and fitness a vibrant and satisfying part of the lives of its members. The company will start with a single fitness center in Oviedo, Florida, a suburb of Orlando. The steps shown in Table 8.2 is the process the company will use to recruit members and it is the method that the in-house staff will follow when people walk into the center and inquire about membership. At times, the process will take weeks to unfold if the employees of Prime Adult Fitness have multiple contacts with a prospect, and at times the process will take only a few minutes as an employee provides the prospect a tour of the facility, answers specific questions, and closes the sale. Prime Adult's sales process is offered only as an example. You can use this example as a template for developing a sales process that fits your business.

Mapping the sales process in the manner shown in Table 8.2 provides a standard method for the employees of Prime Adult Fitness to use, and can be easily taught to new hires. Often, when companies lose an important sale and reflect on what went wrong, they'll find that a key step in the sales process was missed or mishandled. For example, the initial contact may have been mishandled (i.e., a prospect waited at the counter for 10 min until someone spoke to them, and then the person who spoke to them acted hurried or was curt). This is where having a well-thought-out sales process, with accompanying action steps and appropriate employee training, can dramatically improve a company's sales performance.

**Table 8.2. Sales Process (and Implementation Steps) for Prime Adult Fitness**

| | Stage in process | Ways prime adult fitness will support each phase of the process |
|---|---|---|
| 1. | Prospecting (or sales lead) | • Referrals from current members.<br>• Direct mail (targeting households that meet Prime Adult Fitness's demographic profile).<br>• Partnership with Central Florida Health Food.<br>• Partnership with Oviedo Doctor's and Surgeon's Medical Practice.<br>• Downloads from company Web site.<br>• Responses from the company's radio and print advertisements. |
| 2. | The initial contact | • All employees will be provided training in building rapport with prospects.<br>• Prospects are provided an information packet about Prime Adult Fitness.<br>• Radio and print ads will direct prospects to Prime Adult Fitness's Web site, which contains a short video and other promotional material. |
| 3. | Qualifying the lead | • All employees will be trained to assess whether a prospect represents a qualified lead. Prospects that are qualified as good leads will be offered a tour of Prime Adult Fitness's facilities.<br>• If a qualified lead does not join initially, he or she will be contacted by phone as a follow-up three days after the visit. |
| 4. | Sales presentation | • Qualified leads will be provided a facility tour.<br>• Qualified leads will be shown a short film (six minutes) featuring Prime Adult Fitness's facility and programs and the benefits of fitness for older people.<br>• A packet of testimonials will be developed over time and provided to prospects as part of the sales presentation process. |
| 5. | Meeting objections and concerns | • Employees will be trained on how to meet the most common and obvious objections and concerns.<br>• In regard to price objections, a brochure has been prepared that compares (a) Prime Adult Fitness's initial (one-time) enrollment fee and monthly membership fee to other fitness centers and (b) the cost of joining and belonging to a fitness center as opposed to other forms of recreation and entertainment (i.e., boating and golfing).<br>• A similar brochure has been prepared to compare Prime Adult Fitness's amenities to the amenities of other fitness centers. |

*(Continued)*

*Table 8.2.  Sales Process (and Implementation Steps) for Prime Adult Fitness (Continued)*

| | Stage in process | Ways prime adult fitness will support each phase of the process |
|---|---|---|
| 6. | Closing the sale | • All employees will be trained to ask qualified prospects to join. |
| 7. | Follow-up | • Each new member will be contacted by phone 30 days after they join as a courtesy to see how things are going. After that, they will be contacted by phone once a year. Each phone call will also be used to ask for names of referrals.<br>• Prime Adult Fitness will produce a monthly newsletter that will be mailed to each member.<br>• Prime Adult Fitness's staff and employees will be trained to engage members and to thank them for their membership and solicit suggestions for improvement on a continual basis. |

*Source*: Barringer, B. (2009). *Preparing Effective Business Plans*. Pearson Prentice-Hall: Upper Saddle River, NJ

# Step 3: Understand Your Customer's Buying Cycle

An issue that's relevant to how you construct your sales process is understanding the buying cycle of your customer. In short, the buying cycle is the process that customers go through to make a purchase. Once you start engaging a potential customer in your sales process, the customer starts going through a parallel process that culminates with the decision to buy or not to buy. There are five steps in the buying cycle, as shown in Table 8.3.

*Table 8.3.  Steps in Customer Buying Cycle*

| Step in buying cycle | Explanation |
|---|---|
| Awareness | Customer identification of a need and the realization that your business can potentially fill it. |
| Consideration | Customer's evaluation of how your offering meets the need, including an evaluation of offerings from your competitors. |
| Preference/intent | The customer's emotional and logical inclination toward one solution or another, ultimately leading to a purchase decision. |
| Purchase | The action of ordering or buying from your business. |
| Repurchase | The emotional and logical process that (hopefully) leads to repeat business. |

You should learn as much as you can about how your customers pass through this cycle. For example, the length of the buying cycle varies significantly from one industry to another. The buying cycle for low-price consumer products is fast. Consumers normally don't spend much time mulling over what brand of paper towels to buy. In contrast, if you're selling a high-ticket item like a new enterprise software system to businesses, the buying cycle may be fairly long. It may take a business several months to evaluate your system along with the systems of your competitors. The structure of the industry and economic circumstances also make a difference. For instance, if you're trying to sell textbooks or educational software to school districts, the product typically needs to be reviewed by multiple committees consisting of teachers and administrators before a purchase decision is made. You might also hear something like, "We like your product, but don't have the budget to buy right away. We'll reconsider next year." If this is the case, the buying cycle may extend into years.

There are four factors, which can be partially seen in the previous examples, that affect the length of your customer's buying cycle.

- The uniqueness of your product. If your product is unique enough that customers have to be educated before they can make a purchase decision, the buying cycle will be extended.
- The number of people involved. The more people that are involved in the buying decision, the longer it will take.
- Price. The higher the price, the longer the buying cycle.
- Number of competitors. The more comparison shopping that your customers do, the longer the process will take.

So, at the minimum, you should have a good sense of the length of your customer's buying cycle.

Next, you should incorporate knowledge about your customer's buying cycle into how you execute your sales process. The following is each step in the buying cycle and how it impacts the sales process.

- Awareness. This relates directly to how you prospect customers, make the initial contact, and qualify leads. For example, Prime Adult Fitness (the fictitious fitness center for people aged 50 years and older) has a partnership with a local physician's practice. The practice has a large number of patients in the 50+ age range. Short infomercials are shown promoting Prime Adult Fitness on the TV monitors in the waiting rooms. The physicians also periodically refer patients who need to be on exercise program to Prime Adult Fitness. Through this strategy, Prime Adult Fitness is prospecting people who fit the demographic of its target market and the doctors are qualifying leads by sending them people who need to enroll in a fitness program.

- Consideration and preference/intent. These steps relate to the sales presentation and meeting objections and concerns phases of the sales process. In the case of Prime Adult Fitness, its employees are trained to give facility tours, the company has a lively six-minute video that they show prospects, and employees have a brochure available that compares Prime Adult Fitness's initial membership fee and monthly fee to other fitness centers and other forms of exercise. Employees are also trained to engage potential customers by remembering their names, asking them about their families, and making them feel comfortable in other ways.
- Purchase. This relates to closing the sale.
- Repurchase. This step relates to the follow-up stage of the sales process. The likelihood that a customer will repurchase relates directly to the quality of your product or service and the extent to which you follow-up and maintain contact with the customer.

## Step 4: Making Your First Sale

Making your first sale is an exhilarating experience. You can plan all you want, but it's not until you actually make a sale that you know you have a real business. Your first sale will also give you a shot of confidence and pride.

You should view your first sales as more than just making money. You can learn a lot from your first customer or customers. They'll give you insights into how much people are willing to pay for your product or service, how long it takes to close a sale, how easy it is to use your product or service, and so on. Some businesses, depending on the nature of their business, will even ask their first customer or customers if they can call them periodically or visit their homes or businesses to see how their product or service is being used. This approach was utilized in the early days of Intuit, the maker of Quicken, QuickBooks, and TurboTax. Scott Cook, Intuit's founder, would go into stores where Intuit's software was being sold and wait for someone to buy one of his products. He would then ask if he could follow the customer home and watch while the customer installed the software and tried to use it. Cook's approach became known as "follow-me-home" testing and various versions of it have been utilized by many businesses.

Your first sale will also bring to life many of the pieces you've put in place during the prelaunch phase of the First 100 Days plan. You'll now have sales numbers to load into your bookkeeping system, will be collecting sales tax (in some instances) that will have to be passed on to state tax authorities, will be utilizing your office and other resources to make sales rather than just preparing to make sales and so forth.

There are other commonsense things you should do when you make your first sale. You should follow-through as expediently as possible to provide the actual product or service. You should also write your customer a hand-written note thanking them for the business and asking for feedback and for referrals.

There are entire books written on how to make sales, and that topic is beyond the scope of this book. There are three recurrent themes in the books about how to makes sales, however, that you should be particularly mindful of:

- Give yourself a deadline. At some point, every new business has to transition from the prelaunch phase to the postlaunch phase. In this book, we have set the prelaunch phase at 30 days. While your number may be different, you should mark a date on the calendar on when you're going to start selling. If you're product or kservice isn't perfect, in most cases that's ok. You can allow your initial customers to provide you feedback for how to make it better.

- Ask for the sale. While this may seem obvious, some businesses fail because the founder or founders never directly ask for sales. "Ask for the sale" means just that—ask the person who can buy your product to buy it.

- If it's not working, get feedback from others. If you're trying to sell and it just isn't happening, ask for feedback. Politely ask the people who you're trying to sell to why they're not buying. You might also go to other businesspeople, tell him your story, and ask for their advice. Once you've listened to the advice and have regrouped, set a new deadline and start the process over again.

## Step 5: Measuring Results and Reviewing the Sales Process for Improvements

You should put in place mechanisms that allow you to track how effective each step in your sales process is. For example, in the case of Prime Adult Fitness (see Table 8.2), when a prospect phones, sends an e-mail, or walks into their facility to inquire about membership, they should ask the prospect how they become aware of Prime Adult Fitness. This information should be captured in a systematic manner, and be used to determine which forms of prospecting are the most effective. Similarly, when prospects pose objections or concerns, the company's personnel should be trained to remember those objections and concerns and record them in a central place (such as in a notebook accessible by all employees or a public folder on the business's computer network) so they can be evaluated, and responses to the objections and concerns can be formulated and taught to the employees. You should follow a process like this even if you're a one-person company. You should isolate each step of your sales process, determine how you will measure its effectiveness, and then put procedures in place to record the data and periodically review it. The point is to become a business that continually learns and improves. It sounds cliché, but these are the types of qualities that separate successful businesses from unsuccessful ones.

A useful tool that many businesses use to monitor and improve their sales process is to think of it as a sales funnel. At the top of the funnel you have all the people you're prospecting (called "unqualified prospects") and at the bottom of the funnel (many steps later) you have the people who have bought your product or service and received delivery. Over time, you'll learn how many people you need at each stage of the funnel to produce a predictable level of sales. For example, you may find that you need to prospect 1,000 people a month, through a combination of direct mail, online advertising, and direct sales calls to produce 75 people who provide you an opportunity to engage them further. After you shift through the 75, you may qualify 30 as legitimate leads and make your pitch. Ultimately, 12 may say they'll buy your product and 9 will actually follow through and buy. Thinking of your prospects as passing through a sales funnel and measuring results at each stage of the funnel also helps you spot problems and take corrective action quickly. For example, you may find that you're qualifying the same number of leads each month, but your sales pitch is converting fewer actual sales. On investigation, you might find that your main competitor has added a new feature to its product, which is increasing its conversion rate at your expense. You may have to add a similar feature to your product to remain competitive.

The overarching point is that you should think of the sales function of your business in these types of mathematical terms. You should have a sense of how many people you need to prospect and how many people you need to pitch each month to produce a given level of sales. You should also have a sense of the performance of each stage of your funnel. You'll gain these insights by monitoring each step of your sales process on an ongoing basis.

You'll also want to improve conversion rates by sharpening the elements of your sales process. For example, over time, you'll improve your prospecting by learning which forms of advertising work better than others, and the number of people out of the 1,000 you prospect who respond positively may raise from 75 to 90. Similarly, if you improve on your pitch, you may be able to convert a higher number of legitimate prospects to actual sales. The logic is similar for each stage of your sales funnel.

# APPENDIX
# First 100 Days Plan

## Postlaunch (Days 31–100)

### Part 8: *Creating a Sales Process and Your First Sale*

|  | Requirement | Check when done | Result (fill in below) |
|---|---|---|---|
| Step 1 | Creating a Sales Process | ☐ | Recreate Table 8.1 in the textbook for your start-up. (It may be identical to Table 8.1 in the chapter, or you may revise it as appropriate). |
| Step 2 | Implementing the Sales Process | ☐ | Recreate Table 8.2 in the textbook for your start-up, including ways you'll support each phase of the process for your start-up. (If you made changes to the steps in the sales process in Step 1, base the table you create in this step on your changes). |
| Step 3 | Understanding your customer's buying cycle | ☐ | Describe the length of your customer's buying cycle and the implications of the length of your customer's buying cycle on your sales process. Describe how each step in your customer's buying cycle will impact the design of your sales process. |

*(Continued)*

*Part 8: Creating a Sales Process and Your First Sale (Continued)*

| | Requirement | Check when done | Result (fill in below) |
|---|---|---|---|
| Step 4 | Making your first sale | ☐ | Describe the circumstances under which you believe you'll make your first sale. Describe what follow-up, if any, you plan to have with your initial customer or customers. |
| Step 5 | Measuring results and reviewing the sales process for improvements | ☐ | Brief describe how you'll measure the results of your sales process and how you'll use that information. |

# CHAPTER 9

# Marketing

## Introduction

The second step in the postlaunch phase of the First 100 Days Plan focuses on marketing. Marketing is a broader concept than sales. It encompasses all the activities involved with persuading a buyer to purchase a product or service from a seller. Because there are so many alternatives for promoting a business's product or service, marketing is an area in which you need to be careful. If you (a) don't establish a marketing strategy that guides your efforts and (b) aren't aware of the range of options you have, you can easily spend a lot amount of money and get few results. The key is to develop an approach to marketing that is consistent with your business's core mission and is laser-focused on your target market.

Your approach to marketing should also be intimately tied to the seven steps in your sales process. The essence of marketing is to provide a framework—through product, price, promotions, place (or distribution), branding, and so forth—through which a business can effectively prospect customers and close sales. For example, once you launch your business you'll be frequently approached by other businesses that would want to sell you advertising space in their newspaper or magazine or air time on their radio station or TV channel. You should approach these types of solicitations with both your overall marketing strategy (explained later) and your sales process clearly in mind. You shouldn't buy an ad unless you're convinced that the ad is prospecting your specific target market and will result in sales leads that will potentially convert to sales.

There is some trial-and-error that will take place. You may have to experiment some to know what advertising media are the most effective in reaching your target audience, and it may take some time to totally flesh out what your target market is. The overarching point is that you should develop a deliberate and purposeful approach to marketing.

The following are the steps in The First 100 Days Plan covered in this chapter:

| Step 1 | Establish a Marketing Strategy |
|--------|-------------------------------|
| Step 2 | Determine Points of Differentiation |
| Step 3 | Cultivate Reference Accounts |
| Step 4 | Develop a Press Kit |
| Step 5 | Setting Your Price |
| Step 6 | Promotions |
| Appendix | First 100 Days Plan: Marketing |

## Step 1: Establish a Marketing Strategy

A business's marketing strategy is its overall approach to marketing its products and services, which forms the basis of all of its marketing-related activities. It should be consistent with the business's overall mission and values. For example, the mission of Prime Adult Fitness, the fictitious fitness center introduced in the previous chapter, is to "make exercise and fitness a vibrant and satisfying part of the lives of people who are 50 years old and older." The company fervently believes that 50+-year-old men and women who exercise regularly will feel better, live longer, and lead more satisfying lives. Prime Adult Fitness's marketing efforts should reflect these core beliefs. A common mistake that new businesses make is that their marketing efforts are poorly focused. If you and the other people behind your company have strong convictions regarding the value of your product or service, those convictions should be the focal point of your marketing efforts.

How to make this concrete is to write out the marketing strategy for your business. It should be a two- to three-paragraph statement that articulates the overall gist of what your approach to marketing will be. For example, Prime Adult Fitness's marketing strategy is to generate grassroots support and word-of-mouth referrals through a series of marketing tactics that affirm the important of exercise for people aged 50 years and older. This approach has resulted in the forging of partnerships with a health food store and a physician's practice in Prime Adult Fitness's trade area. It has also resulted in training of staff, employees, board members, advisory board members, and even members to make referrals and to convert referrals into new members. What Prime Adult Fitness isn't interested in is superficial ads that reach a general population. Its limited marketing budget is narrowly targeted to reaching the most likely prospects for its fitness center.

## Step 2: Determine Points of Differentiation

Once you have a marketing strategy, you should list the points that differentiate your product or service from your competitors. These points should be emphasized consistently in your marketing efforts. This is a potentially make-it or break-it issue for many businesses. It's hard to get people or businesses to try something new or change their buying patterns and switch from a product they're currently using to a new one. As a result, you have to clearly explain how your product or service is better or cheaper to get people to try it.

The best way to approach this task is to limit the number of points you focus on to two or three to make them memorable and distinct. If you try to emphasize more than two or three points, your customers may not remember the most compelling ones. A useful exercise that helps a business think through the most important points of differentiation is to answer the following question: "The three primary reasons prospects should buy my product or service opposed to my competitors are _____, _____ and _____." Think carefully how you would fill in the blanks.

## Step 3: Cultivate Reference Accounts

Once you have a marketing strategy and have determined your points of differentiation, you should starting putting in place the individual elements of your marketing program. A good first step is to cultivate reference accounts. A reference account is a user of a business's product or service who is willing to give a testimonial regarding his or her experience with the product or service. To obtain reference accounts, new businesses must often offer their products or services to a group of customers for free or at a reduced price in exchange for their willingness to try the product or service and for their feedback. There is nothing improper about this process as long as everything is kept above board and you're not indirectly "paying" someone to offer a positive endorsement. Once the testimonials are collected, they can be used in advertisements, company brochures, on the company's Web site, e-mail newsletters, and by salespeople who are able to tell potential customers about the positive experiences that other customers have had.

The reason reference accounts are so powerful is that endorsement of your business is coming from someone other than yourself. While there is nothing inherently wrong with advertising and similar forms of promotion, people know that ads and promotions are paid for, so they discount them to a certain degree. It is generally much more persuasive when an unbiased third party talks about the merits of your product or service.

It will obviously take you time to accumulate a collection of reference accounts, but you should start right away, even if you have to give away your product or service to obtain your initial testimonials, as previously mentioned. The biggest concern that your initial prospects will have is that your business is new and untested. A testimonial from people who have used your product or service and have been pleased with the results is the most persuasive way to overcome these objections.

## Step 4: Develop a Press Kit

The next step is to develop a press kit. A press kit is a prepackaged set of promotional material for a business (or a person) that is distributed to the media. Media outlets, such as newspapers, magazines, blogs, radio programs, and television shows, use press kits to formulate stories. For example, if you see an article in a magazine about an exciting new start-up, it's very likely that the start-up provided the magazine a press kit and the magazine's editors were intrigued enough that they wrote an article about the start-up. Journalists also draw upon their archive of press kits when events happen and they want to find stories that reflect on the events. For example, if you're starting a company that helps people recover from natural disasters such as floods, hurricanes, tornados, earthquakes, fires, and so forth, if a tornado struck your area and damaged homes and other property, the newspaper might run a story on local businesses that help people recover from tornados.

Businesses often put together a press kit when they launch and then update it periodically. Table 9.1 lists the common elements placed in press kits.

**Table 9.1. Common Elements Placed in Press Kits**

| |
|---|
| • Human interest story about the business's founder or founders. |
| • Human interest story about where the business idea for the company came from. |
| • A press release detailing the current news that has prompted the initial creation or the update of the press kit. |
| • Biography of the founder and other key team members. |
| • Digital photos (on a disk or thumb drive) of the founder, logo, products, and so forth. |
| • Past press coverage. |
| • Testimonials from people who have used your product or service. |
| • Media contact information. For most new business, this will be the business's founder. |

The number one rule for press kits is to include human interest stories. Focusing too much on the features and benefits of their products is a common mistake that businesspeople make when trying to gain attention from the press. Journalists are typically not interested in helping you promote your product or service. Instead, what they prefer is a human interest story about why the business was started or something that's distinctly unique about the start-up. For example, recall Constant Comfort Air Handler, the fictitious company introduced in Chapter 5, Protecting Your Intellectual Property, which produces a portable air handler that is able to maintain a constant air temperature by emitting hot air when the room is too cold and emitting cold air when the room is too hot. Imagine the device was developed by a mechanical engineer, working in his spare time, to help medical doctors in developing countries maintain a steady temperature in the operating rooms of makeshift hospitals that don't have central heat and air conditioning systems. After developing the device for this purpose, the inventor found broader uses for the technology, and has created a version of it to sell directly to consumers. Although your business may not have as dramatic a story as this, make sure to incorporate into your press kit the "human interest" dimension of your business. This is the dimension of your business that journalists are most interested in and will most likely write about.

Your obvious goal in developing a press kit is to encourage the media to help create awareness in your business. Stories written about your business in newspapers or magazine are often the most effective way to generate buzz about your product or service. One outlet for your press kit to be sure to include are bloggers. Often, businesses will get the first stories published about themselves in blogs. If you get mentioned by small blogs, it's easier to get the attention of larger blogs. Once you get mentioned by larger blogs, it's easier to get the attention of magazines and you sort of move up the ladder. The key is to reach out to these media outlets with a professional looking press kit that contains interesting material. Most businesses now develop what's called electronic press kits (EPKs). These are press kits that can be delivered by e-mail.

## Step 5: Setting Your Price

You'll need to set the price for your product or service. Price is an important issue because it determines how much money a business can make. The price a business charges for its product or service also sends an important message to its target customers. For example, Apple Inc. positions its desktop and laptop computers as innovative, state-of-the-art products that are high quality, easy to use, and interface seamlessly with other Apple products. This position in the market suggests the premium price that Apple charges. If Apple advertised innovative, state-of-the-art desktop and laptop computers and charged a bargain basement price, it would send confusing signals to its customers. Its customers would wonder, "Are Apple products high quality or aren't they?" The low price also wouldn't generate the type of financial returns that Apple needs to continue innovating in its product categories.

The first thing to do in determining your price is to survey the prices of your competitors. For example, say you're located in Southern California, and you're opening a foreign language academy that will focus on teaching Spanish to businesspeople. Your business will be called Golden State Language Academy. You should put together a chart that lists the prices of your local competitors, along with the most popular software-based foreign language platforms, such as Rosetta Stone. Your chart should include a column for your prices, which will be empty until you evaluate the prices of your competitors, a column for your local competitors, and a column for online alternatives. Your initial chart would look something like that shown in Table 9.2.

*Table 9.2. Prices for Spanish Instruction (In Your Business's Trade Area Plus the Most Popular Online Program)*

| Hours of instruction for face-to-face instruction | Golden state language academy | Average fees of direct competitors in your trade area | Online competitors rosetta stone |
|---|---|---|---|
| 15 hours | | $420 | |
| 20 hours | | $560 | |
| 30 hours | | $840 | |
| 40 hours | | $1,120 | |
| 60 hours | | $1,680 | |
| Level for online instruction | | | |
| Basic | | | $179 |
| More Advanced | | | $299 |
| Most Advanced | | | $399 |

This information will enable you to set your prices, based on the manner in which you're differentiating yourself from your competitors. For example, in regard to your direct competitors, if you believe the quality of your instruction, the convenience of the hours your offer, and the friendliness and patience of your tutors place you a cut above your competitors, you may be able to charge a premium price. The online competition is a little trickier. Rosetta Stone is a well-established competitor with a premium brand, and there are similar online alternatives. The way most face-to-face foreign language services differentiate themselves from online competitors is by offering "immersion" courses that can be completed in one to two weeks, and by offering personalized instruction. If you're a busy executive prepping yourself for a trip to Peru, a Spanish-speaking country, and a large sale hinges on your ability to interact effectively with your Peruvian customer, you may not have the time or patience to self-teach yourself Spanish via the Rosetta Stone system. A two-week immersion course, taken in a classroom setting, may be a much better fit for your needs. The instructors in a classroom setting may also be best equipped to help you fine-tune the specific sales pitch you'll be delivering in Spanish.

Most experts warn start-ups to resist temptation to charge a low price for their product or service in the hope of capturing market share. This approach can win sales but generate little profit. In addition, most consumers make a price–quality attribution when looking at the price of a product. This means that consumers naturally assume that the high-priced product is also the better-quality product. If a business charges low prices for its products, it sends a signal to consumers that the product is of low quality regardless of whether it really is.

Remember, too, that the price you're able to charge is a function of (a) the objective quality of your product or service and (b) the perception of value that you create in the minds of your consumers relative to competing products in the marketplace. This is one of the reasons that reference accounts are so important. If you're opening a Spanish language instruction service, and you're targeting businesspeople, imagine how powerful the following testimonial would be if you put it on the front page of your Web site and the person writing the testimonial was highly credible:

> "I enrolled in the two-week Spanish immersion course at Golden State Language Academy. I had a little trouble catching on, and the instructors stayed after class with me for several days to help me out. By the end of the course, I was confident I could make the trip I planned and converse with my Spanish prospects. I made a one-week trip to Mexico City, and landed a $450,000 contract for my business. That contract is just the boost my company needed, and I've already scheduled two more trips to Mexico. Thank you Golden State Language Academy!"

A final consideration in pricing is that you have to cover your overhead and make a profit. This topic will be covered in more depth in Chapter 12, which focuses on tracking and managing your business's finances, but ultimately you must make a profit. Price is the only element of your marketing mix that produces income—everything else is an expense. As a result, you have to price your product or service in a manner that not only makes sense in the marketplace, but also returns to you a profit.

## Step 6: Promotions

You should approach promotions cautiously. It's in the area of promotions that a business owner can spend a lot of money for very little results, or a small amount of money for large results.

The first rule of thumb is to consider as many alternatives as possible before settling on the techniques you'll use to try to prospect potential customers. In some cases, the choices will be clear. For example, if you plan to launch a Web site to sell large-size men's shoes, the only practical way to reach your audience may be through pay-per-click advertising (more about this option later). For example, type the phrase "large size men's shoes" into the Google search engine, and you can see the paid ads for large-size men's shoes Web sites at the top and to the right of the organic search results. In other instances, the best choice or choices may be unclear, and it may take some guidance or trial-and-error method to find the best alternative. For example, there isn't an obvious answer for how to best promote Golden State Language Academy, the fictitious Spanish language tutoring service referred to earlier. The place to start is to try to discern where the company's target market, Southern California businesspeople who want to learn Spanish, would most likely look if they wanted to find a service to learn Spanish.

The second rule of thumb for selecting ways to promote your business is to think creatively. A problem that many new business owners have is that they're familiar with the most expensive ways to advertise—print and media advertising—and are less familiar with more cost-effective alternatives. A large print ad in a major magazine can cost up to $25,000, for example, which typically far exceeds the advertising budget of most new businesses. There are alternatives that are significantly less expensive—from writing a blog to handing out brochures—which take time and effort rather than financial resources.

The following are the most common tactics and techniques for promoting your business. In most cases, a business will rely on a combination of these techniques rather than just rely on one or two. Serendipity and luck also play a role. For example, a new business may have a feature article written about it by a magazine or newspaper, as a response to sending out its press kit. This type of occurrence can bring more visibility to a business than a score of paid advertising can.

### Print and Media Advertising

Print and media advertising runs the gamut from television ads to direct mail to posting flyers on grocery store bulletin boards. Don't rule out any particular form of advertising until you know more about it. For example, in many cities, there is inexpensive air time available on certain cable channels during nonpeak times of the day. A company such as Golden State Language Academy may find that one of its best choices is to produce a short infomercial that introduces its service, provides examples of its instruction, and includes testimonials from past students. The cable channels have profiles of when certain demographic groups are most likely to be watching, so the spots could be run during the times when businesspeople are tuned in. The spot could also include a 1-800 number and a Web site address for people to enroll in future classes.

The type of advertising a business selects hinges largely on whether it is targeting a national audience, like an e-commerce site that plans to sell large men's shoes, or a local clientele, like Prime Adult Fitness, the fitness center for people aged 50 years and older that will have a single location. Some of the items discussed in Chapter 6, Establishing a Professional Image, are subtle forms of advertising that all businesses should take advantage of. For example, you should distribute your business cards liberally and list your company in both online and print directories, particularly those directories (like Google and Bing) that are free.

In general, new businesses that plan to target a local clientele normally avoid television, newspaper, and magazine advertising because of the costs involved, with the exception of the infomercial example provided above. Some businesses find radio advertising to be effective if the listening audience reflects the demographic they're trying to reach. For example, a new financial planning service may sponsor or buy ads on a radio show that focuses on providing investment and retirement planning advice. Classified ads, either in local newspapers or online, remain effective in many instances. Some businesses work hard to get listed on Web sites that review local businesses, like Yelp! As mentioned in Chapter 6, a business's signage can be its most important form of advertising.

If you're trying to reach a national audience, the primary challenge is how to fight through the noise and reach your specific target market. There are several ways to do this. There are literally thousands of magazines that target narrow niches. Another option is to advertise in an industry trade journal, if it's a good fit. A directory of trade associations (which publish trade journals) is available through Weddle's at http://weddles .com/associations/index.cfm. Many trade associations also sponsor trade shows where new businesses can gain visibility and display their products.

### Internet Advertising

An increasingly effective way for all new businesses to prospect customers is to utilize Internet advertising. The primary mechanism for small businesses is pay-per-click programs, which are provided by Google, Bing, Yahoo!, and other online firms. Google has two pay-per-click programs—AdWords and AdSense. AdWords allows advertisers to buy keywords on Google's home page, which triggers text-based ads at the top and to the right-hand side of the organic results when the keyword is used. So if you type "Spanish Language Software" into the Google search box, you'll see ads from several vendors that have Spanish language software programs to sell. Many businesses report impressive results utilizing this approach, presumably because they are able to place their ads in front of people who are already searching for information about their products. Google's other pay-per-click program is called AdSense. It is similar to AdWords, except that advertiser's ads appear on other Web sites rather than Google's home page.

There are businesses that rely almost exclusively on pay-per-click advertising to promote their products. For example, 2BigFeet (www.2bigfeet.com) sells shoes up to size 20 for men and 14E for women. People find out about 2BigFeet when they search for unusual sized shoes on Google and other search engines. If you'd like to know more about Google AdWords or AdSense go to www.google.com/adwords and/or www.google.com/adsense. Bing and Yahoo have similar programs.

Online advertising extends to social networking sites, such as Facebook. Advertising on Facebook is quite different from pay-per-click advertising. People go to Facebook primarily to socialize with family and friends, rather than to look for a product. As a result, most businesses use Facebook to build relationships rather than generate immediate sales. This can be done by offering useful information and advice, posting coupons, announcing sales, or even wishing people "Happy Birthday" or "Happy Anniversary." The appeal of advertising on Facebook is that you can reach a very narrowly targeted audience. (Facebook gets information on its users in various ways, including scanning their profiles and studying the Facebook groups they join). Facebook allows you to select demographics such as country and city, age range, gender, interests, and more. As a result, you could literally target men aged 18–36, who live in Oklahoma, and are Oklahoma City Thunder (an NBA team) fans. You can learn more about Facebook advertising at www.facebook.com/ads.

You can also generate interest in your business and products through blogging and participating in social media sites (such as Facebook, Twitter, and LinkedIn) as discussed in Chapter 7, Establishing an Online Presence.

### Public Relations

One of the most cost-effective ways for a new business to achieve visibility and promote its products or services is through public relations. Public relations refers to efforts to establish and maintain a company's image with the public. The major difference between public relations and advertising is that public relations is not paid for—at least directly. The cost of public relations is the effort that a business makes to maintain its press kit and to network with journalists, blog authors, government officials, and others to try to incent them to say and write positive things about their company and its products. Public relations may also involve spending money on sponsorships, like sponsoring a community event or a small league baseball team.

The most common public relations techniques are as follows:

- Press release
- Public service announcement
- Event sponsorship
- Traditional media coverage (such as stories in newspapers and magazines)
- Social media coverage
- Articles in industry periodicals, such as trade journals
- Monthly newsletter
- Open houses and facility tours (for bigger companies)
- Civic, social, and community involvement.

### E-mail Newsletter and e-mail Marketing

As mentioned in Chapter 7, Establishing an Online Presence, building an e-mail list of prospects and customers is a smart thing to do, for the purposes of distributing a monthly or quarterly e-mail newsletter and for e-mail marketing.

The purpose of creating an e-mail newsletter is to stay in contact with prospects and customers, and by doing so add to your sales funnel. A newsletter shouldn't blatantly solicit business—that's not its purpose. Instead, it should be "chatty" in tone and provide interesting tidbits about your industry, your company, one or more of your customers, and so forth. The following is a list of information often found in company e-mail newsletters:

- One feature article (not focused specifically on your product or service)
- Highlights of a new innovation in your industry
- Testimonial from a satisfied customer
- Human interest story about something connected to your company or industry
- Quick introduction to one of your employees (depending on whether you have employees)
- Special offers or coupons
- Upcoming promotions or sales

The key is to provide enough interesting content that people open the newsletter and read or at least scan it. This can take a lot of work, so you'll need to weigh the advantages of producing a newsletter against the opportunity costs of your time. You don't necessarily have to produce all the content yourself. For any industry, you can type into Google "free _____ articles." There are people, just like you, trying to get noticed, and in some industries one technique for getting noticed is to write articles about specific topics and allow others to reprint them for free.

### E-mail Marketing

E-mail marketing is reaching out to prospects via e-mail. It involves using e-mail to send ads, request business, solicit sales, or to build loyalty through e-mail newsletters or similar means. You have to be careful to make your e-mail pitches tasteful, so your prospects and customers don't feel like they're being spammed or your messages don't end up in junk e-mail folders.

The major advantages of e-mail marketing is that it's inexpensive, you can track the exact number of your messages that were opened, and almost half of American Internet users check their e-mail at least once a day. A well-known technique that e-mail marketers use is to send their messages between 1:00 am and 5:00 am in the morning, so the message will appear at the top of the recipients e-mail list when they open their e-mail in the morning. Some businesses obtain a high rate of their e-mail being opened by offering valuable discounts to customers who open the messages and are then privy to the discounts.

The main disadvantage of e-mail marketing is that you run the risk of annoying prospects and customers who are adverse to e-mail solicitations. Deliverability is another issue, as e-mail filters are becoming better at sniffing out solicitation e-mails.

Similar to asking prospects and customers to "opt-in" to receive a monthly or quarterly e-mail newsletter, you should ask permission before you send e-mail solicitations. Many prospects and customers will give it to you, because they're hoping to receive e-mail messages with coupons or discount offers.

# APPENDIX

# First 100 Days Plan

## Postlaunch (Days 31–100)
### Part 9: Marketing

| | Requirement | Check when done | Result (fill in below) |
|---|---|---|---|
| Step 1 | Establish a marketing strategy | ☐ | Articulate your business's marketing strategy in two to three paragraphs. |
| Step 2 | Determine points of differentiation | ☐ | List two to three primary factors that differentiate your product or service from competitors. |
| Step 3 | Cultivate reference accounts | ☐ | Describe how you would cultivate reference accounts for your business. |
| Step 4 | Develop a press kit | ☐ | Describe the items you would include in your press kit. Also list the first five media outlets or journalists (specific names) that you would send your press kit to. Explain the rationale for your selections. |

| | Requirement | Check when done | Result (fill in below) |
|---|---|---|---|
| Step 5 | Setting a price | ☐ | Set the price for your primary product or service. Describe the rationale for the price you selected. |
| Step 6 | Promotions | ☐ | Describe the specific promotions mediums you would use, and the rationale behind your choices. |

# CHAPTER 10

# Operations

## Introduction

This portion of the First 100 Days Plan focuses on how you will produce your product or service and service your customers. There are two things to be mindful of as you approach this section. First, operations is the heartbeat of a business. It will consume the majority of your time and attention. The goal is to create a repeatable and teachable process that involves purchasing inputs, converting the inputs into outputs, and then delivering the outputs to customers. Creating and adhering to a pattern like this is why a restaurant like McDonald's is able to deliver to you a piping hot meal in just a few minutes, even if its busy and is run by what appears to be a group of teenagers. Over time McDonald's has established a fine-tuned approach for converting inputs (meat, cheese, lettuce, tomatoes, potatoes, buns) into outputs (hamburgers, cheeseburgers, fries) and then delivering them to you (either across the counter or at the drive-up window).

It's your job to do the same for your business. You need to develop a fine-tuned approach for converting the inputs in your business into outputs, and then seamlessly delivering the outputs to your customers. This thinking applies even if you're opening a one-person business like a tax preparation service. Your inputs might be your time, your expertise, and the computer hardware and software you use to figure your clients' tax returns. Your outputs are completed tax returns that are accurate, that fully adhere to IRS regulations, and that minimize your clients' tax liability.

The second thing to be mindful of as you approach this section is to focus on how your operations help create the points that differentiate your business from your competitors. It's easy to say, for example, that your business will provide the highest level of customer service in your trade area, but how exactly does that happen? Will you be providing your employees special training? Are your facilities superior to those of your competitors? Will you fulfill orders in a superior way? Will you interact with customers in ways that your competitors don't? These issues are fleshed out and executed on through the operations function of your business.

The following are the steps in The First 100 Days Plan covered in this chapter:

| Step 1 | Operations Model and Procedure |
|--------|-------------------------------|
| Step 2 | Purchasing Inputs |
| Step 3 | Managing Inventory |
| Step 4 | Distribution |
| Step 5 | Customer Service |
| Appendix | First 100 Days Plan: Operations |

## Step 1: Operations Model and Procedure

At the time your business launches, you should have a firm grasp on the operational details of how you'll convert inputs into outputs and deliver them to customers. Ultimately, you'll be judged by your customers by how much value your product or service delivers, which is an operational issue. If your product is judged to be of medium or poor quality or the service you deliver isn't all that it should be, your business will have little chance of being successful.

There are two useful ways of thinking through and depicting the operations of your business. The first is by framing your operations in terms of "back stage," or behind-the-scenes activities, and "front stage," or what the customer sees and experiences. Table 10.1 provides an example of how this is done. Imagine you're opening a coffee shop, much like a Starbucks or Caribou Coffee, named Pine Tree Coffee. Your coffee shop's operations are shown in Table 10.1 using the front-stage/back-stage metaphor.

### Table 10.1. Operations Model for Pine Tree Coffee

| Back stage (behind the scenes operations activities) |
| --- |

- *Staff Selection.* The staff and employees will be carefully selected. Along with the skills they need to perform their jobs, staff members must be able to demonstrate passion for coffee and relate to customers in a professional, thoughtful, and caring manner.

- *Training.* All new hires will be assigned a trainer/mentor. The new hire will work the same schedule as the trainer/mentor during the first four weeks of employment (which is also the length of the probationary period). On the fourth Friday morning of every month, all employees will meet for 60 min prior to the opening of the shop for special training and updates on company policies and events.

- *Coffee, Other Beverages, and Pastries.* All coffee, tea, and specialty drinks will be prepared in-house, by Pine Tree Coffee baristas. Bottled drinks will be purchased from vendors on an approved vendor list. Pastries will be made by a local bakery, and delivered to Pine Tree Coffee twice a day (5:30 am and 11:00 am).

- *Coffee Beans.* All coffee beans and raw ingredients needed to produce coffee, teas, and specialty beverages will be purchased from an approved vendor list. All brewed coffee and coffee beans sold at Pine Tree Coffee will be Fair Trade Certified.

- *Customer Retention.* One the most important ingredients to Pine Tree Coffee's success will be repeat business. Patrons need to feel like they are welcome and their business is appreciated. Staff at all levels will be trained to offer this type of attention. The staff will be encouraged to remember the names of regular customers and let people know they are missed when they don't come in for a while. It is the personal connection to employees, and to the coffee house experience, that keeps people coming back to an establishment like Pine Tree Coffee.

- *Branded Supplies.* Branded supplies, such as Pine Tree Coffee Cups and napkins, will be purchased once a month by the First Assistant Manager.

- *Generic Supplies.* Generic supplies, such as paper products, dishwasher soap, and cleaning products, will be purchased on the 15th and 30th of every month at Costco, by the First Assistant Manager.

- *Advertising.* Purchase ads only to advertise catering service.

- *QuickBooks.* All financial transactions, including money coming in (cash receipts, credit card payments, debit card payments) and money going out (bills, rent, utilities, payroll, payroll taxes) will be recorded in QuickBooks at the end of each business day.

- *Operations Manual.* An operations manual will be prepared to document and articulate the day-to-day operational procedures of the coffee shop.

- *Emergency Plans.* Emergency action plans, policies, procedures, and rules have been established and will be part of each employee's training regime and are documented in the operations manual. There will be no ambiguity or indecision when an emergency occurs. If a customer needs medical attention, there is a robbery, or there is an incident that puts the safety of customers and Pine Tree Coffee personnel at risk, all employees will know the procedure to follow.

*(Continued)*

*Table 10.1. Operations Model for Pine Tree Coffee (Continued)*

| Front stage (what the customer sees and experiences) |
| --- |
| • *Hours of Operation.* Pine Tree Coffee will be open from 5:30 am until 7:30 pm daily. |
| • *First Contact and Processing Orders.* All customers will be greeted—by name if they are regulars. Employees will be trained to engage customers while at the same time keep the line moving. The POS system in the shop will record the order. Nonbarista sales (such as bottled drinks and pastries) will be handed to the customer on a tray by the cashier at the time of sale. The baristas will receive orders for coffee, teas, or specialty drinks (which includes the customer's first name) on a digital display. When the order is filled, the customer's name will be called out to deliver the order. The customer will be thanked when the order is delivered. |
| • *Ambience.* The ambience of Pine Tree Coffee is relaxed and unhurried. During down times, employees will be trained to circulate in the shop, and engage customers if it seems appropriate. Soft music will be present in the shop at all times. Pine Tree Coffee's rich "coffee house" atmosphere will be maintained throughout the day. |
| • *Cleanliness.* A rigorous schedule for busing tables, general pickup, sweeping floors, and servicing restrooms will be maintained. |
| • *Community Involvement.* Take active role in supporting community events within a three-mile radius of Pine Tree Coffee. Specifically, buy sponsorship for July 4 5 K run, support nonprofit art gallery on Oak and 12th street, allow full-time employees to donate up to 4 hours "on the clock" to support Labor Day weekend craft and art show in Messenger Park, and donate coffee and pastries to, on a case-by-case basis, to nonprofit neighborhood events. |
| • *Custom Cups.* Design and use custom coffee cups that feature explanations of specialty coffees served by Pine Tree Coffee or provide a portrait and short bio of one of Pine Tree Coffee's baristas. |
| • *Coffee Bar.* Feature a "coffee bar" on Thursday afternoons from 5:00 pm to 7:00 pm, which allows patrons to taste and experience coffees from around the world. The most popular coffees will be featured on Pine Tree Coffee's "Customer's Choice" menu on a rotating basis. |
| • *Catering.* Tasteful signs are present throughout Pine Tree Coffee's facility advertising the company's catering service. Every Wednesday, the napkins that are distributed will feature a promotion for Pine Tree Coffee's catering service. |
| • *Gift Cards.* Gift cards will be available for purchase at the cash register stations. |

If Pine Tree Coffee were a real company, the list of both back-stage and front-stage activities would be more extensive, to flesh out the operational policies and daily activities of the company. Developing a back-stage/front-stage operations model is a useful exercise that you should complete for your business.

The second way to illustrate how a product or service is produced is to produce an operations flow diagram. An operations flow diagram shows the key steps in the production of a product or the delivery of a service. It's a particularly useful exercise for manufacturing start-ups. Often, the operations flow diagram also depicts how the company intends to improve the flow of activities in its operations compared with industry norms. For example, IKEA is the Swedish furniture company known for its brightly colored furniture and its approach of requiring customers to assemble their furniture (in exchange for a lower price). Figure 10.1 demonstrates IKEA's operations flow. Traditional furniture manufacturers tend to complete more of the activities themselves, whereas IKEA has opted to outsource the assembly and delivery of its furniture to its customers. In IKEA's case, its operations flow diagram paints a fairly clear picture of how the company operates.

Although both the back-state/front-stage approach and the operations flow diagram describe how a company's operations work, there are additional operational details you'll have to work out. Many are nontrivial

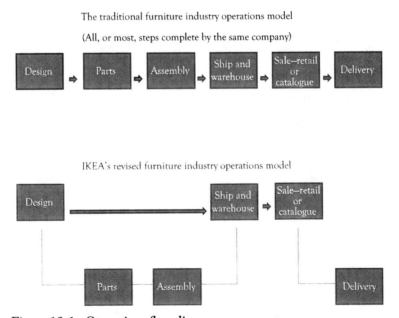

Figure 10.1. Operations flow diagram.

issues, and make a big difference in terms of a business's efficiency and effectiveness. Examples include:

- How your inventory will be stored and how frequently it will be turned over. For a company such as Pine Tree Coffee, this involves the place where its excess coffee beans and other raw ingredients will be stored, how often orders for new ingredients will be placed, how will the ingredients be shipped, who will open the shipments and replenish the supplies, and so forth.

- A description of the length and nature of your product or service's production cycle. For Pine Tree Coffee this involves when they pay for raw ingredients (and other supplies), how long it takes to convert an order of supplies into sales, when they get paid, and so forth. What Pine Tree Coffee will want to do is to negotiate net 30 or 60 days for payment of raw ingredients (coffee beans). Because their product sells quickly (restaurant coffee sales) and they are paid by the customer at time of purchase, they can generate income from brewed coffee sales and bean coffee sales before they pay for the ingredients.

- An explanation of where bottlenecks are likely to occur in your manufacturing process or service delivery and how these will be handled. For Pine Tree Coffee (and all coffee shops), the bottleneck is the morning rush.

- An explanation of how quality control is maintained. For Pine Tree Coffee, this may mean periodically surveying customers or tasting samples of brewed coffee to ensure quality standards.

You should make a list of similar operational-level issues for your business and determine how you will address them.

## Step 2: Purchasing Inputs

Purchasing inputs (supplies) is an important activity. The inputs for a business like Pine Tree Coffee consist of coffee beans, other raw ingredients that go into beverages, branded supplies (like cups with the Pine Tree logo), and generic supplies (like paper towels and dishwasher soap). While it will take some time to get it right, the ultimate goal in purchasing is to buy the exact amount you need, at the lowest possible price, and have it delivered just when you need it.

The topics that will be discussed in this section include: purchasing policies, the ordering system, and receiving orders.

## Purchasing Policies

Most businesses designate one employee (at the beginning it's usually the owner) to do the purchasing. That person's task will be to select vendors, negotiate price, quality expectations, and delivery schedule, and try to obtain payment terms that are most favorable. The payment terms on which a business negotiates is a key issue. As mentioned earlier, if a business such as Pine Tree Coffee can get 30 days or 60 days net payment terms (which means they don't have to pay for the supplies they order for 30 to 60 days after delivery), they can generate income from the supplies before they pay for them (thus strengthening their cash flow).

A company's purchasing policy should also be fully consistent with its overall approach to business and the values it wants to express. For example, Pine Tree Coffee will only sell Fair Trade Certified Coffee. This policy, even though it means that Pine Tree Coffee will pay more for ingredients than many of its competitors, is reflective of the company's core values and is an important part of its purchasing policy.

Purchasing is also somewhat of an art. You have to anticipate demand so you have enough supply available to meet demand. Some retailers have to anticipate demand months in advance so they can purchase sufficient supply to have their shelves stocked when their peak selling season arrives. Purchasing also depends on the inventory on hand. For example, if Pine Tree Coffee has a slow month and its inventory of coffee beans and other ingredients isn't depleted as rapidly as anticipated, it may delay its routine monthly order by 15 days to allow its inventory to be drawn down. Conversely, if it has a particularly busy month, it may need to move up its next order date.

### Ordering System

You should develop a formal ordering system. Rather than ordering supplies on an ad hoc basis, you should place orders at regular intervals (every other Friday afternoon, for example). Generally, the steps in a formal ordering system are as follows:

- Quickly survey suppliers (to see who has the best price–quality combination)
- Place the order (with an agreed upon delivery date)
- Receive the order
- Check the order for accuracy
- Pay the supplier.

The extent to which this process takes time and effort depends on the situation. For example, Pine Tree Coffee may establish an arrangement with a local restaurant supply company to deliver a certain quantity of supplies every month on an automatic reorder basis. In this case, very little work is involved after the initial contract is negotiated. Conversely, the company may send its buyer to Central America to negotiate directly with growers of coffee beans the best possible price and delivery terms. In this case, the effort would be extensive.

Supplies are typically ordered via a purchase order. A purchase order is a formal request to the vendor or supplier to deliver certain materials or supplies according to the terms and prices agreed upon. Purchase orders help businesses document and keep track of ordering activity, and elucidates the terms of an order to both parties. A purchase order should include the following information:

- Your company name, address, telephone number, fax number, and e-mail address
- Your business's logo
- Name of the vendor or supplier you're ordering from
- Type of product or service being ordered
- Quantity desired
- Price
- Delivery terms.

### Receiving Orders

A packing list will accompany orders you receive. Check the order to make sure it matches the packing list. Note any discrepancies and report them to the vendor immediately. File the packing list. If you haven't been invoiced for the order, make sure to check the packing list against the invoice when it arrives.

You should work with your vendors and suppliers to make sure orders arrive when it's least disruptive to the normal routines of the business. Pine Tree Coffee, for example, would not want routine orders arriving during the 6:30 am to 8:30 am timeframe, when its employees are busy serving the morning rush.

## Step 3: Managing Inventory

Inventory refers to raw materials (like coffee beans), goods in process (such as product halfway through the production process), and finished goods (such as clothing on a rack in a clothing store). Each form of inventory is necessary, but represents money tied up in assets that haven't yet generated income. This section focuses on two topics: inventory management and inventory control.

### Inventory Management

Inventory is a two-edged sword. You want to have sufficient inventory on hand to provide your customers options and to guard against running out if demand exceeds forecasts, but you don't want to have so much inventory that you're unnecessarily tying up your money. If you purchase too much inventory, there is also the chance that some of your inventory will go out of fashion or lose its appeal if a newer version of the product appears on the market. Inventory must also be stored and insured, and in some cases, like cut flowers or perishable food products, must be refrigerated or maintained in some other special manner.

There are additional challenges in inventory management. Examples include:

- Maintaining a wide assortment—but leaving enough space for the most popular items. For Pine Tree Coffee, this means finding the balance between having a wide variety of coffees available while at the same time keeping in stock the most popular blends.

- Increasing inventory turnover—but not sacrificing service. Pine Tree Coffee can speed up its lines during the morning rush, and increase its inventory turnover, by limiting selection and not spending as much time helping customers make choices. The tradeoff is less special service.

- Lowering the price via volume discounts—but risk getting stuck with slow-moving inventory. Pine Tree Coffee may strike a deal with a new grower and get coffee beans at a discount, but may regret the decision if the new grower's coffee turns out to be a slow seller.

### Inventory Control

There are two levels of inventory control systems: manual systems and more sophisticated computer-enabled systems.

Manual systems rely on business owners visually inspecting their inventory to determine if additional inventory is needed. This approach may be adequate for a business like Pine Tree Coffee, where the owner or manager could visually examine the inventory at the end of each day and determine when new inventory needs to be ordered. Some businesses also use fairly unsophisticated paper inventory control systems. For example, the baristas may record the date and number of drinks ordered on a clipboard for less popular selections. This information may tell the purchasing manager that a certain type of coffee bean will need to be reordered every 90 days, instead of every 30 days as is the case for popular selections.

The second option is to adopt a point-of-sale system (which is controlled by the cash register) that allows you to track usage of inventory and alerts you to when new inventory needs to be ordered. Most systems also produce sales data that can be very helpful to businesses. For example, if Pine Tree Coffee adopted a robust point-of-sale (POS) system, the system could not only help it manage its inventory, but could tell it what products are selling best at what time of day. A business can also run "tests" using POS systems to help maximize sales. For example, Pine Tree

Coffee might try offering a 20% discount on lattes if purchased before 7:00 am. The POS system could not only help determine if the discount increased latte sales before 7:00 am, but if the increase in sales was enough to compensate for the lower net margin per sale.

There are similar computer-controlled inventory management systems for manufacturing business, which enable firms to monitor their inventory of component parts as they manufacture and assemble the finished product. If your business might benefit from this type of system, contact an inventory management system vendor for more information.

## Step 4: Distribution

Distribution is the activity that moves a business's product or service from its place of origin to the consumer. There are three topics that are discussed in this section: selling direct, selling through intermediaries, and blended distribution strategies.

### Selling Direct

Many businesses sell directly to customers. For a company like Pine Tree Coffee, the bulk of its sales are across the counter in its coffee shop and via catering events, which are direct sales. Most retail stores and e-commerce Web sites sell direct. For example, Apple sells computers through its company-owned stores, and Amazon.com sells books and other items through its Web site.

For businesses where customers pay for the product or service at the time of sale, distribution isn't an issue. If a company like Pine Tree Coffee starts selling branded coffee beans online or through catalogs, then distribution becomes more of an issue. The company has to decide how to fulfill and ship the orders it receives. Traditionally, businesses like Pine Tree Coffee have managed the fulfillment and shipping of orders themselves. There are now other options. For example, Pine Tree Coffee could contract with a fulfillment and shipping company such as Shipwire (www .shipwire.com) to receive, warehouse, and ship its coffee beans. Pine Tree Coffee would still make the sales through its Web site, but the site would be electronically monitored by the fulfillment and shipping company, and when an order came in it would be shipped by the fulfillment company within the same day to the customer. It could even be shipped in a box labeled Pine Tree Coffee, which contains a Pine Tree Coffee shipping list along with the product. Of course, there is a fee for this service, but an increasing number of small businesses are opting in favor of this option rather than managing the fulfillment and shipping of orders themselves.

If Pine Tree Coffee decided that it wanted to sell its branded coffee beans through local and regional grocery stores, and manage the sales and distribution function itself, it would need to field a sales force to call on local and regional stores, and then create a system for getting its coffee beans to the stores and ensuring that the stores maintained an adequate supply. Its responsibility might not stop there. The stores through which it sells may require help to "support" their sales. An example of how Pine Tree Coffee might do this is by sending employees to the stores to hand out samples of its brewed coffee.

### Selling Through Intermediaries

Instead of selling direct, some businesses sell through intermediaries, such as distributors, wholesalers, and manufacturing representatives. For example, rather than trying to field a sales force to call on local and regional grocery stores, Pine Tree Coffee could sell through a distributor or a wholesaler, who would call on the stores on its behalf. The distributor or wholesaler could then help Pine Tree Coffee design a system for getting its coffee beans to the stores and ensuring that the stores maintained an adequate supply. In many instances, the distributor or wholesaler would take delivery of the coffee beans that Pine Tree Coffee contracted for from producers, and then deliver the beans to the appropriate stores.

Service providers can also sell through intermediaries. Hotels, for example, sell their services (rooms) across the check-in counter, through their Web sites, and through their telephone reservation systems. They can also sell through intermediaries, such as travel agents, tour operators, airlines, and so forth. For example, if you were planning a trip to New York City to see a Broadway play, you could book your flight, rental car, and hotel through Travelocity or Expedia, or many similar services. In this instance, Travelocity and the others are acting as intermediaries for the service providers. This option is becoming more prevalent for small companies and even freelancers. For example, in some locations, consumers can connect with service providers such as massage therapists, personal trainers, and childcare providers through online services like Angie's List (www.angieslist.com) and Redbeacon (www.redbeacon.com). In these instances, the online services are acting as intermediaries. Many freelancers, particularly graphic designers and computer specialists, book jobs through online sites such as Guru (www.guru.com) and ODesk (www.odesk.com). Again, the online sites are acting as intermediaries.

### Blended Distribution Strategies

Businesses of all sizes also utilize blended distribution strategies, where they sell direct plus sell through intermediaries. For example, many businesses sell their product via their Web site (direct) and also through distributors who help them land shelf space in retail stores (intermediaries). If handled awkwardly, this approach can cause what's called "channel conflict." Channel conflict can occur when a business sells online (capturing all the profits itself) and also wants retailers to sell its products through their stores. The retailers may be less motivated to carry or push the business's product thinking that customers might see the product in their store and then go online to buy it. Despite this potential complication, many businesses sell both online and through distributors and manage the process.

## Step 5: Customer Service

Most small businesses cannot compete with larger competitors on price or breadth of product offering. As a result, a competitive advantage is typically gained through a high level of customer service and a variety of other factors. An emphasis on customer service can be seen in Pine Tree Coffee's operations model (see Table 10.1). In both its back-stage and front-stage operations, providing a high level of customer service is clearly a priority. Two customer-service-related topics are addressed here: customer service basics and building customer relationships.

### Customer Service Basics

The first step in establishing a high level of customer service is to make it part of the culture of your business. You do this by emphasizing customer service from day one. You also do it by hiring employees who have the personality and skill sets to deliver high levels of customer service.

The following are examples of ways in which you can "implement" a desire to deliver high levels of customer service in your business. You should evaluate each of these possibilities and adopt the ones you think are the best fit for your business. You should also seek out suggestions for other ways to implement a high level of customer service for your customers or clientele.

- Develop measurements of high levels of customer service. One problem with customer service is that it's hard to quantify, so if you can come up with methods to actually measure the level of customer service you're delivering, you can get better at it. For example, some companies will count the number of problems their customers have that they're able to solve.
- Emphasize customer service in interactions with vendors, customers, and employees. A "mindset" of high customer service extends beyond customers. It extends to everyone that a business interacts with.
- Establish customer service focused routines. Many businesses establish routines they are followed consistently. For example, in its operations model, one of the activities Pine Tree Coffee has thought through carefully is first contact with customers and processing orders. According to Table 10.1, "All customers will be greeted—by name if they are regulars. Employees will be trained to engage customers while at the same time keep the line moving." Further down the narrative reads, "When the order is filled, the customer's name will be called out to deliver the order. The customer will be thanked when the order is delivered." Note how customer service considerations are embedded into these routines.

• Recognize that customers are human beings. Act on the knowledge that customers are human beings, and that most (if not all) human beings value attention and a caring attitude. As a result, look for occasions to spend extra time with customers or go the extra mile.

### Building Customer Relationships

One trap that's easy to fall into is that when you make a sale, you quickly move on to the next prospect, without spending time building a relationship with the customer you just acquired or customers you already have. This is typically a mistake. The lifeblood of most businesses is repeat business from existing customers. The following are ways to build relationships with customers in hope of encouraging repeat business.

• Thank customers for their business. This sounds like an easy step, but it's often overlooked. You should put a program in place to thank customers (at the time of sale or on special occasions, like their birthdays) for their business. Something as simple as sending a customer a thank you note or a birthday card with a $15 gift certificate to a local restaurant can help build relationships.

• Engage customers on a regular basis. This can be done through talking to customers if they come to your place of business, or can be accomplished through an e-mail newsletter or via social media such as Facebook or Twitter.

• Address customers by name. There is no better way to establish rapport with a customer than to address him or her by name. It sends a message to the customers that he or she isn't just a potential sale but is a person of value and worth.

• Offer a customer reward program. Customer reward or loyalty programs work well for many types of businesses. The most effective programs offer graduated rewards, so the more the customers spend, the more they earn. It's better to offer in-kind rewards (such as a free unit of your product or service for every 10 purchased) than an external reward, such as cash.

# APPENDIX
# First 100 Days Plan

## Postlaunch (Days 31–100)

### *Part 10: Operations*

| | Requirement | Check when done | Result (fill in below) |
|---|---|---|---|
| Step 1 | Operations model and procedures | ☐ | Recreate Table 10.1 for your business |
| Step 2 | Purchasing inputs | ☐ | Describe your purchasing policy, the ordering procedures you'll use, and how you'll receive shipments (if applicable). |
| Step 3 | Managing inventory | ☐ | Describe how you'll manage inventory (if applicable) |
| Step 4 | Distribution | ☐ | Identify whether you'll sell direct, through intermediaries, or utilize a blended approach. Describe the specifics of your approach. |
| Step 5 | Customer service | ☐ | Identify the initiatives you'll utilize to provide a high level of customer service. Describe, to the extent possible, how you'll "implement" these initiatives. |

# CHAPTER 11

# Managing a Business's Money

## Introduction

In the postlaunch stage, it's very important for a business to manage its money prudently. Money is fuel—it's the resource that allows your business to open its doors every day. Having adequate money on hand will help your business grow and prosper. Not having sufficient money on hand will do just the opposite. It will cripple your business and make it less likely that your business will grow and reach its financial potential.

Fortunately, there are techniques that help businesses manage their money carefully and shrewdly. It's important that your business develops sound money management practices from the outset. Many businesses fail to reach their full potential simply because they do not manage their cash and their finances correctly.

The following are the steps in The First 100 Days Plan covered in this chapter:

| Step 1 | Paying Bills |
|--------|--------------|
| Step 2 | Sending Invoices |
| Step 3 | Collecting on Overdue Invoices |
| Step 4 | Providing Customers Credit |
| Step 5 | Managing Cash Flow |
| Step 6 | Estimated Tax Payments |
| Appendix | First 100 Days Plan: Managing a Business's Money |

## Step 1: Paying Bills

Paying bills won't be among your favorite activities, but it is something you have to do. There are two considerations in paying bills. First, you should pay your bills on time. It's not only the right thing to do, but it will also strengthen your reputation and will incent vendors and others to "want" to do business with you. Second, you should pay your bills in a manner that lets you best manage your cash flow. The goal is to maintain sufficient cash to meet your immediate needs. To do this, business owners must sometimes pay bills by credit card, for example, rather than by check to avoid depleting their cash balance below a certain amount. The credit card can then be repaid when cash is more plentiful.

There are three primary methods a small business can use to pay its bills: checks, credit cards, and online.

### Paying Bills by Check

The most popular option for paying bills is checks. Credit cards and online payments are gaining, but most businesses maintain a checking account and pay some or all of their bills by check. There are several advantages of paying by check. First, paper checks still offer businesses several days of "float," which is the time between when the check is written and when it is cashed. This window is narrowing, however, and float time isn't as long as it used to be. Second, paper checks provide an accounting advantage, since the check itself provides physical proof of a transaction. Finally, checks can be stopped, via a stop-payment order, if anything is found to be amiss between the time the check is written and it is cashed.

The disadvantage of checks is that the physical process of writing checks, placing them in envelopes, putting postage on the envelopes, and getting the envelopes to the post office is more expensive and more of a hassle than paying by credit card or online in many instances. An added advantage of electronic payment options is that recurring bills can be paid automatically.

### Paying Bills by Credit Cards

The second option is to pay bills by credit card. If you pursue this route, you shouldn't use your personal credit card, even if you keep good records and the business pays you back for business-related purchases. It's not a clean way of running a business. Even though your business is new, it might not be as hard to obtain a business credit card as you might think. Most banks have programs to accommodate small businesses, and are generally eager to get your business. This is particularly true if you already have a checking account and a merchant bank account (which allows you to accept credit cards) at a bank.

The biggest advantage of paying by credit card is that it helps you manage your cash flow. You can use your card to pay bills when your revenues are low or expenses are high, and then repay the card when the opposite conditions exist. For example, many retail stores have cyclical selling cycles. They may be adding inventory for a holiday season, such as Christmas, and rely on credit cards or a bank line of credit to help fund their inventory. After Christmas is over, they can repay the line of credit or credit cards through their added receipts. In the early months and years of a business, you may also need credit cards to simply smooth out your monthly cash flow. Properly used, credit cards can be a tremendous asset for a small business.

If you do get a business credit card, try to get one that offers reward points, such as a Staples card, that will allow you to accumulate points and get discounts on office supplies. You can also automate the payment of many routine bills by placing them on your credit card account.

There are three things to be cautious about in using credit cards to pay bills. First, not everyone you purchase from will take credit cards, so you still have to maintain a traditional checking account. Second, you should discipline yourself, to the extent possible, to not maintain a balance on your credit card from month to month to avoid interest charges and accumulating debt. Finally, if you get multiple cards for the same account and distribute them to your employees, do this causally. You can generally set up controls on cards handed out to employees, such as spending limits and restricting the card to certain types of purchases or even specific vendors.

### Paying Bills Online

The third option is to pay bills online, by charging the payments to a checking account, credit card account, or an electronic account such as

PayPal. The number of businesses that accept online payments is growing rapidly. In most instances, even landlords are becoming sophisticated enough that they accept online payments for rent.

The primary advantage of paying online is that you can do it anytime anywhere, as long as you have access to the Internet. You can also make changes, such as switching from charging a bill from your checking account to your credit card account. This degree of flexibility helps you manage your cash flow. You can also set up automatic payments, similar to what you can do if you pay by credit card. In addition, online payments are typically free. This advantage avoids the postage cost that's normally required if you pay by check.

It's also getting easier to begin paying online. Almost every bank now offers an online system that allows you to access your checking and savings accounts to pay bills and keep track of account activity. It's actually cheaper for banks to process online payments than to process checks. As a result, it is likely that banks will continue to push online payments and will make it an increasingly attractive option for paying bills.

# Step 2: Issuing Invoices

Unless you're starting a business where your customers pay you at the time of purchase (like a restaurant or retail store), you'll need to issue invoices to the businesses and people who buy your product or service. An invoice is the list of the products or services provided to a customer and the payment that is due. There are three things to be mindful of when issuing invoices: setting up an invoicing system, items that need to be included in invoices, and payment methods you'll accept from your customers.

## Setting Up an Invoicing System

The first thing to consider in invoicing is to set up an invoicing system. You should bill or invoice customers within one to two business days of when you delivered the product or service. Most of the standard bookkeeping systems, such as Quickbooks and Freshbooks, have built-in invoicing capabilities. If you're not using an electronic bookkeeping system, you should develop a system where you invoice promptly and keep track of outstanding invoices and their due dates.

### Items That Need to be Included in Invoices

You can develop your own format for invoices, or use a standard template. Table 11.1 includes a list of the information that must be included in invoices.

**Table 11.1. Information That Must be Included on Invoices**

| | |
|---|---|
| 1. | The customer's name. |
| 2. | Your company's name. |
| 3. | The invoice number. Invoices must be issued in the proper numerical order. |
| 4. | The date. |
| 5. | Delivery date for goods or services. |
| 6. | The name and description of the products or services sold. |
| 7. | Total Invoice Amount. The amount should include price + sales tax (if applicable) + delivery charge (if applicable) – any price reductions and discounts (if applicable). |
| 8. | Payment terms. You can state "payment due upon receipt" or offer terms such as "payment due within 30 days of receipt." Just recognize that if you offer terms, such as payment due within 30 days of receipt, you probably won't get paid until close to the 30 day deadline. |

You must keep copies of the invoices you issue. This step is critical for financial accounting and tax purposes.

### Payment Methods You'll Accept

You'll need to make a decision regarding the payment methods you'll accept. The choices you have for paying bills (see Step 1) are the same choices that you can offer your customers to pay you. The choices are by check, credit card, or via an online payment.

Getting paid by check (or cash) is an option that nearly all businesses offer their customers. The advantage of cash or check is that there are no transaction costs involved. You deposit the full amount your customer pays you. It will involve a trip to the bank, but normally is well worth it as opposed to paying 3–5% fees to accept payment by credit card or debit card. Some businesses only accept payment by cash or check, primarily to avoid fees. While this sounds good, it may act as a deterrent to sales. Your clients may prefer to pay by credit card so they can manage their cash flows. If you don't offer that option, they may go elsewhere.

You can accept credit card and debit card payments if you set up a merchant bank account, as described in Chapter 4, Bookkeeping and Financial Management. There are low-cost options available to start-ups and small businesses that you might want to consider, such as Square, which charges a 2.75% flat fee. Make sure you fully understand what the 2.75% flat fee means. It means that if you sell something for $100, and accept payment via Square, you'll only get $97.25. Square will take $2.75 as a processing fee. The same holds true for accepting credit cards and debit cards. The fees will vary depending on the circumstances. PayPal is another option.

You can accept payments online. There are many reliable services that can set this up for you. Ask your bank for a referral. Accepting payments online works out particularly well if you offer a recurring service. Instead of invoicing your clients once a week or once a month by mail, you can invoice them by e-mail and they can then pay online using a credit card or their bank account. The payments will go directly into your merchant account, which means you'll get paid quicker. You can also set it up so your customer gets an e-mail reminder 2–3 days before the payment is due.

## Step 3: Collecting on Overdue Invoices

For most small business owners, collecting past due accounts is one of the most unpleasant tasks of owning a business. Studies show that the longer past due bills go unpaid, the less likely it is that they will be paid, so it's important to have a process in place for addressing past due accounts as soon as they become past due.

There are many books, articles, and Web sites that help business-people develop systems and routines for collecting past due accounts. The high points will be covered here. There are two facets to addressing past due accounts: how to avoid accounts running past due to begin with, and how to collect on past due accounts.

### How to Avoid Accounts Running Past Due

There are several things you can do to try to avoid accounts running past due. If you're selling a high ticket item, you can do credit checks on clients prior to consummating sales. Federal law requires that prior to conducting a credit check, you must seek the permission from your client in writing. Once you get the permission, you can run a credit check through one of the three main credit reporting agencies, which include Experian, Equifax, or TransUnion, or if you need a more extensive report through Dun & Bradstreet. Credit checks on businesses outline the business's payment history and help predict future payment behavior. You should have a standard policy for the threshold you use to qualify an individual or business as having acceptable credit. Before you start conducting credit checks, you should familiarize yourself with the federal Fair Credit Reporting Act and the applicable state laws. For example, if you reject a client based on a credit report, you need to disclose this to the person, as well as the name, address, and phone number of the credit reporting agency that gave you the negative information.

You can also offer incentives to your customers to pay early. For example, you could offer a 2% discount for accounts paid within 10 days. This approach not only generates cash for you quickly but also helps avoid the possibility of that account eventually running past due.

### How to Collect on Past Due Accounts

There are many approaches and theories on how to collect past due accounts. It's a difficult task, because you want to get paid while at the same time preserve the relationship with the customer. Table 11.2 contains a list of generally recommended steps for collecting past due accounts.

Through the collection process you also have the option of offering your customer a payment plan to resolve the outstanding account, or even offer to settle for less than the full amount if you fear your customer is experiencing financial distress and you may get nothing if the customer files bankruptcy. If you offer a payment plan and the customer accepts your offer, the terms of the plan should be clearly spelled out in a letter that you mail to the customer. You should include in the letter a

**Table 11.2. Generally Recommended Steps for Collecting Past Due Accounts**

| | |
|---|---|
| 1. | Add a service charge for running late. Make sure the charge is sufficient enough that it stings some. If it's not, you may inadvertently encourage customers to string out their payments, if the service charge they pay you is less than the interest charge they would pay their credit card company to pay you and carry the debt. Check with local authorities to make sure you don't exceed your state's usury statutes and federal law. |
| 2. | If the account remains past due, make a phone call or visit your customer to discuss the past due account. Remember, you want to preserve the relationship. In the initial call, you might want to say something like, "Just checking to make sure you have the invoice we sent you. We appreciate the fact that you normally pay on time, so were wondering if you might have misplaced the invoice or didn't receive if for some reason?" This approach allows your client to save face and say the invoice will be paid and the call can end without confrontation. |
| 3. | If #2 doesn't work, make a series of additional calls or send reminder letters, with escalating rhetoric. Many businesses use letters to document their collection attempts. |
| 4. | If the account remains unpaid, your remaining options are to turn it over to a collection agency or file suite in small claims court. If the past due amount exceeds the amount you can sue for in small claims court, you'll need to retain an attorney to file a lawsuit to collect the account. |

place for your customer to agree to the terms and then ask that the letter be returned to you with the acknowledgment. Include a self-addressed stamped envelope for the return.

# Step 4: Providing Customers Credit

Many small businesses launch and vow to never extend credit to their customers. This approach works if your customers pay at the time of sale. Examples of businesses that fit this description are retail stores, restaurants, and service businesses, such as dry cleaners and hair salons, where you pay for the service at the time it's delivered. Businesses that invoice their customers face a different set of dynamics. While you can send invoices that say "Payment due upon receipt," the reality is that in many industries you must offer your customers the ability to pay within 30 days or in some cases 60 days to be competitive. In these instances, you're essentially offering your customer credit between the time you deliver your product or service and the time your product or service is paid for.

Other industries require participants to offer credit for longer terms. If you're manufacturing an expensive machine or software product, for example, you may need to offer your customers the ability to pay for the purchase by making installment payments over a year or more.

This section covers both contingencies: offering your customers the ability to pay within 30 or 60 days and offering your customers the ability to pay via installments.

### Offering Your Customers the Ability to Pay Within 30 or 60 Days

Businesses that invoice customers typically offer payment terms of 30–60 days, without an interest charge. There are two reasons why businesses do this. First, it incentivizes sales by offering customers the flexibility in terms of when they are required to pay. Even a 30-day window offers customers an advantage in managing their cash flows. Second, in many instances, accepting payment within 30 days is a normal way of doing business. For example, some customers (whether they are individuals or other businesses) only pay bills once a month. As a result, they may receive an invoice, and depending on the timing of the invoice, pay 30 days later even if they maintain a policy of paying on time. This is why many businesses accept credit cards, even though there are fees involved. If a customer pays by credit card, you get your money almost immediately. You also shift the repayment risk to the credit card company.

### Offering Your Customers the Ability to Pay via Installments

In some industries, businesses offer their customers credit terms, and allow them to pay for a product or service over an extended period. If you do this, you become a provider of credit, and must comply with a range of regulations that govern the process of offering credit. Regardless of the industry, the following are points to consider before deciding to offer credit. There are both pluses and minuses to offering credit.

- The option of offering credit enables customers to focus less on price, and has the potential to generate greater sales.

- Extending credit ties up your money. Unless a business acquires loans and then quickly sells them to a bank or finance company, it will tie up money and force the business to find other sources of money to manage its own operations.
- If a customer defaults on a loan, a business can lose money or become distracted by going through the collection process.
- Before extending credit, a business should ask itself if it has a significant business need to offer credit. If you're selling an expensive machine or software product to other small businesses, for example, extending credit may be the thing that incentivizes the majority of your customers to do business with you. In contrast, if your business is selling to Fortune 500 firms, they may take advantage of your credit if you offer it, but it may have no bearing on their decision of whether or not to purchase from you.

In most cases, new businesses only offer credit if there is a sound reason to do it. In these instances, the need or the desire to offer credit is generally factored into the business's plan, and the resources required are part of the business's overall financial requirements that are funded by investors or supplied through other means. Rarely does a business offer its customers credit unless it's an integral part of the business's competitive strategy.

If a business does offer credit and charge interest, it should establish policies for determining the creditworthiness of customers (including asking customers to complete a formal application for credit) and put in place standard criteria for accepting or rejecting loan applications. It should also become familiar with laws that regulate offering credit. For example, the laws that regulate consumer credit include the following:

- The Truth in Lending Act
- The Fair Credit Billing Act
- The Equal Credit Opportunity Act
- The Fair Credit Reporting Act
- The Fair Debt Collection Reporting Act

There may be additional regulations in specific jurisdiction, so the legality of offering credit should be thoroughly checked out. If a business offers credit to customers, it should check with an attorney to elicit help in establishing credit policies and in complying with applicable federal, state, and local laws. There are additional considerations. For example, if you're executing a long-term credit agreement with a corporation or partnership, you may want to require that the shareholders or partners offer personal guarantees for the loan. In addition, if you're loaning money for something that can be secured, like a piece of equipment or machinery, you'll typically want to secure the loan with a lien on the property you're selling.

Instead of offering installment loans, some businesses offer their customers a trade account, which is an open line of credit for the purchase of the product or service they sell. For instance, if you open a business that sells auto parts to companies that operate large fleets of car, trucks, or buses, you may set your best customers up on trade accounts where they can charge up to a certain amount of money in parts before they are required to make payment. In this instance, the business is usually charged a service fee or interest charge on the average amount of credit outstanding for a given month.

## Step 5: Managing Cash Flow

A business must always be sure that it has enough money in the bank to meet its payroll and cover its short-term obligations. The practice of doing this is called cash flow management. There is a difference between earning income and having cash. A business can literally have a million dollars in income, but if its income is tied up in accounts receivable it may not be able to meet a $20,000 payroll. This is why almost any book you pick up about starting and growing a business stresses the importance of properly managing your cash flow.

The reason that cash flow challenges are so prevalent is that there is a natural lag between when businesses spend money and when they earn income from the money they spent. Often, equipment must be purchased and new employees must be hired and trained before the increased customer base generates additional income. This lag produces cash flow challenges, particularly for new businesses.

This section focuses on five topics. The first three topics—speeding up the process of collecting on outstanding invoices, techniques for holding off paying bills as long as reasonable, and methods for adding to cash and minimizing expenses—focus on how to improve your cash flow. The fourth topic focuses on preparing cash flow projections. The fifth topic centers on surviving cash flow shortfalls.

### Speeding Up the Process of Collecting on Outstanding Invoices

There are two to three ways to improve your cash flow. The first is speeding up the process of collecting on outstanding invoices (or receivables). Techniques for accomplishing this are provided in Table 11.3.

**Table 11.3. Techniques for Speeding Up the Process of Collecting Outstanding Invoices**

| | |
|---|---|
| 1. | Collect money at the time of sale if possible. |
| 2. | Issue invoices promptly. |
| 3. | Deliver invoices by e-mail rather than via the postal service. |
| 4. | Make it extremely easy for your customers to pay by accepting credit cards and offering online payment options. |
| 5. | Offer a cash discount—say 2%—for accounts paid within 2 days. |
| 6. | Impose a penalty for accounts that run past their due date. |
| 7. | Offer discounts to customers who pay their bills regularly. |
| 8. | Follow-up immediately on accounts that run past due. |
| 9. | Collect money upfront, in the form of a deposit or prepayment, if possible. |

The overarching goal is to generate cash as quickly as possible and to reduce the lag between the costs of producing a product or service and when you are paid.

### Techniques for Holding off Paying Bills as Long as Reasonable

The second way to improve your cash flow is to hold off on paying bills as long as is reasonable. Table 11.4 outlines techniques for accomplishing this:

**Table 11.4. Techniques for Holding off Paying Bills as Long as is Reasonable**

| | |
|---|---|
| 1. | Take full advantage of supplier and creditor payment terms. If a payment is due in 30 days, don't pay it until on or shortly before the 30th day. |
| 2. | Use electronic funds transfer to make payments on the last day they are due. This practice allows you to remain current with your suppliers and creditors, while keeping control of your cash as long as possible. |
| 3. | Carefully evaluate your suppliers and vendor's offers of discounts for early payments. They may provide you a chance to reduce costs, if your cash situation is okay. |
| 4. | Don't always focus on the lowest price when choosing suppliers. It may be worth it to pay a little more if the supplier will give you 60 days to pay your bills. |

In many respects, what you're collectively trying to do in Tables 11.3 and 11.4 is ironic. You want to get paid right away but at the same time find ways to delay paying others for as long as you can. This is the nature of business. As long as what you're doing is within the scope of the agreements you have with both your customers and suppliers, you're simply executing good cash flow management tactics.

### Methods for Adding to Cash and Minimizing Expenses

The third way to improve your cash flow involves a grab bag of techniques. Running credit checks on customers (if appropriate in your industry) helps you avoid servicing customers who pay late. If you have outdated inventory or equipment that you're not using, sell it and place the money in your cash reserves. Finally, minimize expenses where you can. Many businesses bootstrap elements of their initial operations to conserve cash. Bootstrapping is finding ways to minimize expenses (and avoid having to raise money) through creativity, ingenuity, thriftiness, cost-cutting, and any means necessary. Table 11.5 provides examples of bootstrapping methods.

### Preparing Cash Flow Projections

When you first launch your business, you should prepare cash flow projections on a weekly or monthly basis. An accurate cash flow projection will alert you to foreseeable cash flow shortfalls. Your projections will hinge largely on the timing of your income and expenses, and how effectively

*Table 11.5. Examples of Bootstrapping to Minimize Expenses and Conserve Cash*

| |
|---|
| Buy used instead of new equipment |
| Coordinate purchases with other businesses |
| Hire interns |
| Lease equipment rather than buying |
| Share office space or employees with other businesses |
| Buy items cheaply, but prudently, through discount outlets or online auctions such as eBay, rather than at full-price stores |
| Avoid unnecessary expenses, such as lavish office space or furniture |
| Minimize personal expenses |

you manage the steps previously outlined. You'll get better at projecting the amount of cash you'll have on hand as your business matures. The factors that will be most helpful to you in making accurate projections are

- your customer's buying cycles;
- your customer's payment habits;
- your own ability to identify upcoming expenditures;
- your own ability to identify upcoming sales;
- your vendor's patience in accepting payment from you;
- the timing of major expenditures;
- your ability to account for seasonal sales fluctuations.

A cash flow projection (for a week, month, or any other period) starts with the amount of cash you currently have on hand. You then add the cash you'll take in from all sources, including normal operating activities, investing activities (including the sale of assets), and financing activities (including money from investors or from a lender). You then subtract the cash you'll need for normal operating activities, investing activities (including the purchase of assets), and financing activities (including paying dividends to investors and making payments to creditors). The net figure will show you whether your cash balance will increase or decrease as a result of the activities during the period. If cash will go to zero or below, you should recalculate your projection to see exactly what day it will go to zero or below, and then make appropriate plans (see the following section). You should never be caught totally unawares. During the initial months of your business, you should figure your cash flow on either a weekly or monthly basis. If you're using a high-quality bookkeeping system, like Quickbooks, there will be functionality within the system to help you watch your cash balance and monitor your cash flow.

### Surviving Cash Flow Shortfalls

There may come a time when you project that you'll experience a cash flow shortfall. This doesn't necessarily mean that your business is failing or you're not a good money manager. Often, the faster a firm grows the more pressing its cash flow challenges become.

The thing not to do is panic. Fortunately, there are normal, everyday business practices that you can utilize to manage through a cash flow shortfall. Several of the most common techniques are discussed in the following text.

First, if you feel that at some point you may find yourself in a cash flow bind, arrange for a line of credit at a bank, or make sure your business credit card has a generous credit limit and allows for cash advances (without exorbitant fees). The time to arrange the line of credit is before you need the money. Bankers are typically skeptical of businesses who say they're doing well, but are in the midst of a cash crisis and need cash "now."

Second, turn to your suppliers. If your suppliers view you as a good long-term customer, they'll often help you through a cash flow bind by extending the time you have to pay them. Some vendors also offer vendor credit. Vendor credit (also known as trade credit) is when a vendor extends credit to a business in order to allow the business to buy its product or services up front but defer payment until later. Both alternatives help you bridge the gap between acquiring resources to generate cash and actually getting paid. Third, consider factoring. Factoring is a hybrid method for obtaining cash. It's a financial transaction whereby a business sells its accounts receivable to a third party, called a factor, at a discount in exchange for cash.

A final alternative is to ask your best customers to accelerate payments. Explain the situation that you're in, and if necessary offer a discount for early payment. If your customers find value in your product or service, they may be willing to help you withstand a temporary cash flow shortfall.

## Step 6: Estimated Tax Payments

Another factor involved in managing money is paying taxes on time. A good money manager should never be caught off guard with a large income tax obligation. It's an expense you should plan for and be prepared with taxes are due.

A business's owners are required to pay federal income tax quarterly, rather than once a year, if they expect to owe at least $1,000 in federal

*Table 11.6. Filing Dates for Estimated Tax Payments*

| Estimated tax due | For income received |
|---|---|
| April 15 | January 1 through March 31 |
| June 15 | April 1 through May 31 |
| September 15 | June 1 through Aug 31 |
| January 15 | September 1 through Dec 31 |

income tax (for the year) from their interest in the business. The amount is $500 for corporations. Remember, partnerships, subchapter S corporations, and limited liability companies do not pay income tax per se. Instead, their income is "passed through" to their owners who pay taxes on their portion of the entity's income on their personal tax returns. C Corporations, which are less common for news businesses, do pay taxes.

If you are filing as a sole proprietor, a partner in a general or limited partnership, a shareholder in a subchapter S corporation, or a member in a limited liability corporation, you should use Form 1040-ES Estimated Tax for Individuals, to file your quarterly return. If you are filing as a corporation, you should use Form 1120-Estimated Tax for Corporations, to figure the estimated tax.

To figure your estimated tax, you must figure your expected adjusted grow income, taxable income, taxes, deductions, and credits for the year. You want to estimate your income as accurately as possible to avoid penalties.

The filing dates for estimated tax payments are shown in Table 11.6.

There is an important exception for new businesses. You generally do not have to pay estimated quarterly taxes if your business did not owe any tax during the previous year (which would obviously be the case for a new business). If you think you'll be profitable during your first year in business, it's still a good idea to make estimated tax payments or set aside money for taxes, so you won't be hit with a large tax bill on your first annual return.

# APPENDIX
# First 100 Days Plan

## Postlaunch (Days 31–100)

### Part 11: Managing a Business's Money

| | Requirement | Check when done | Result (fill in below) |
|---|---|---|---|
| Step 1 | Paying bills | ☐ | Describe the process your business will use to pay bills. |
| Step 2 | Sending invoices | ☐ | Describe the process, if applicable, that your business will use to issue invoices. |
| Step 3 | Collecting on overdue invoices | ☐ | Describe your business's policy for collecting overdue invoices and accounts. |
| Step 4 | Providing customers credit | ☐ | Report whether your business will offer credit. If it will, elaborate on your credit policy. |
| Step 5 | Managing cash flow | ☐ | Describe how your business will monitor and manage its cash flow. Be specific. |
| Step 6 | Estimated tax payments | ☐ | Report whether your business will be subject to quarterly estimated tax payments. Report when the payments will be due. |

# CHAPTER 12

# Hiring Your First Employee

## Introduction

Hiring your first employee is a big step for a new business. If you're hiring just one employee you're doubling the size of your business, and if you're hiring more than one employee you're doing more than that. Hiring an employee is an investment in your business. If you handle it correctly, it can provide your business a big boost. If you do it wrong, it can set you back and cause all kinds of headaches.

You should approach hiring employees in a contentious manner. Be mindful of the fact that you're dealing with people and their lives. If you hire someone and it doesn't work out, it not only causes problems for you but also for the person you have hired. Also, be careful not to hire someone simply because you're overwhelmed and desperately need help. You should step back and carefully think through the type of person you need, what his or her job description will be, and how the person you hire will fit into the strategic vision for your business.

Hiring is also an area in which you need to be careful about following the rules. There are federal, state, and, in many cases, local tax and labor laws you'll need to comply with. You'll need to bone up on these rules and regulations—they are unique to employers. While this chapter provides an overall introduction to the process of hiring your first employee, it's just a start. Your state and local Chambers of Commerce are excellent sources of information for additional questions you might have.

The following are the steps in The First 100 Days Plan covered in this chapter:

| Step 1 | Establish a Budget for the Position |
|--------|-------------------------------------|
| Step 2 | Write a Job Description |
| Step 3 | Draft an Employee Manual |
| Step 4 | Recruitment, Interviewing, and Selection |
| Step 5 | Complying with Regulations Pertaining to Having Employees |
| Step 6 | Independent Contractors versus Employees |
| Step 7 | Hiring Your Spouse, Children, or Other Family Members |
| Appendix | First 100 Days Plan: Hiring Your First Employee |

## Step 1: Establishing a Budget for the Position

The first step in hiring is to establish a budget for the position. There are three financial components to hiring an employee: base salary or hourly wage, additional employer-related costs (such as workers' compensation insurance), and benefits (if you offer any). The mistake that many first-time business owners make is thinking that if they hire someone for $40,000 a year, it will cost $40,000 per year. It actually costs more than that to employ someone for a base salary of that amount. The following are the three components to which it actually costs to hire an employee.

### Base Salary or Hourly Wage

The first component to compensation is base salary or hourly wage. To come up with this number, you should have a clear idea of what the employee's responsibilities will be. You can then either ask other business owners what the normal pay range is for an employee with those responsibilities, or do some direct research. If you go the direct research route, a good place to start is Salary.com (www.salary.com). Salary.com is a Web site that provides a wealth of salary information about jobs both locally and nationally. For example, according to Salary.com, the medium salary for an entry-level accountant in Stillwater, OK is $39,522 per year. You can also go to job boards like Monster.com to see what other employers in your area are willing to pay for an employee similar to the one you'd like to hire.

Trade associations often disseminate salary information for common jobs in their industries. Both your local and state Chambers of Commerce are also good sources for employment-related information.

You'll need to decide whether to pay your employee an hourly wage or a salary. According to the Fair Labor Standards Act (FLSA), which governs most jobs, employees are either "exempt" or "nonexempt." Nonexempt employees are normally paid by the hour and are entitled to overtime pay if they work more than 40 hours per week. Exempt employees, who are generally paid a salary, don't get overtime pay. The pay you offer for a job is your call, with one exception. Nonexempt employees must be paid at least the applicable Federal minimum wage for the number of hours worked. Additional information about this distinction between exempt and nonexempt employees is available at the U.S. Department of Labor's Web site at www.dol.gov.

For practical purposes, most businesses pay employees in career-oriented jobs a salary while other employees are paid an hourly wage. For example, a salesperson would normally be paid a salary while a call center employee would be paid an hourly wage.

### Additional Employer-Related Costs

There are three additional employer-related costs associated with having employees, which are required by law. The first cost is workers' compensation insurance (if the business has three or more employees). As described in Chapter 3, Getting Up and Running, all employers are required to provide workers' compensation insurance for employees (but not for independent contractors). Rules vary by state. Most small businesses buy workers' compensation insurance through a private insurance carrier. Some states have state funds.

The second cost is Social Security (FICA) and Medicare tax. As described in Chapter 4, Bookkeeping and Financial Management, this is a tax paid by both the employer and employee. You must withhold the employee's share of Social Security and Medicare tax from the employee's paycheck. You must then pay the employer's share. The formula for determining how much is withheld is described in Chapter 4.

The third cost is Federal Unemployment Tax (FUTA). The employer is responsible for paying this tax—it is not withheld from the employee's paycheck. Again, the method for determining the amount to withhold is provided in Chapter 4.

## *Benefits*

Benefits are a voluntary expense and are offered at the discretion of the employer. The trade-off is attracting and retaining high-quality employees versus cost. The most common benefits offered are health insurance, life insurance, dental and vision insurance, sick leave, vacation pay, and a retirement account. The employee generally pays a portion of health, life, dental, and vision insurance.

Combined, the additional employer-related costs and benefits can add 10–30% to the cost of an employee's base salary. The total cost, which is base pay + additional costs + benefits, is the total cost associated with hiring an employee.

Your budget should include the direct costs plus any additional costs associated with the employee. There may be initial costs, such as relocation expenses and training, which must be figured into the year 1 budget for the position.

# Step 2: Write a Job Description

A job description is a list or a narrative that explains the tasks and responsibilities associated with a specific job. It's important to have a formal job description for the position you'll be hiring for several reasons. First, it helps you think through the tasks and responsibilities that the job will consist of. Second, it enables you to better explain the job when conducting interviews. Third, it helps the person who is ultimately hired know what is expected. Finally, it helps you craft your employment ad.

To write a job description you can use a template or design one of your own. Templates are available for free via Microsoft at http://office. microsoft.com/en-us/templates, through many local and state Chambers of Commerce, and through other sources. Most job descriptions include the following information:

- Job title
- Job description (brief summary of the job)
- Job responsibilities

- Other tasks
- Name of supervisor
- Monthly or yearly salary range or hourly wage
- Skills needed (such as communication skills, computer skills, must be able to meet deadlines)
- Years of experience in a related job or field required
- Educational background required.

Be careful to not set some of the conditions for employment, such as educational background required, too high or you may inadvertently exclude qualified candidates.

## Step 3: Draft an Employee Manual

The third step is to draft an employee manual. While this might seem like a large task, it is something that can be done in an afternoon, and can be added to and improved over time.

The best way to approach drafting an employee manual is to utilize a template or electronic wizard that walks you through the process. Many state Chambers of Commerce have employee manual templates or wizards they distribute for free. You can also conduct an Internet search, which will reveal other sources.

There are two reasons that it's important to have an employee handbook. First, it documents your business's policies regarding employee-related issues, such as absences, breaks, dress code, benefits, performance reviews, and so forth. Second, it provides protection against lawsuits. A business is on much firmer ground if it has written policies pertaining to issues such as arriving at work on time, personal time off, sick leave, maternity leave, lunch breaks, and so forth. To take advantage of this protection, when you hire employees you should provide them a copy of the employee manual and ask them to sign an acknowledgment that they were provided the manual.

A sample of topics included in a typical employee manual is provided in Table 12.1. It may take some time and experimentation to flesh-out each of these topics for your business, but over time you should develop a manual that includes at least these items:

*Table 12.1. Sample of Topics Included in Employee Manuals*

| | |
|---|---|
| Absences | Holidays |
| Attendance | Jury Duty |
| Breaks | Lunch Periods |
| Communication Policy | Maternity Leave |
| Confidentiality | Military Service |
| Continuation of Medical Benefits (COBRA) | Performance Reviews |
| Dismissal | Probationary Period |
| Dress Code | Sexual Harassment |
| Drugs and Alcohol | Sick Leave |
| Equal Opportunity | Termination |
| Family Medical Leave Act | Vacation Time |
| Health and Life Insurance | Workers' Compensation |

# Step 4: Recruitment, Interviewing, and Selection

Once you establish a budget for a position, write the job description, and put together an employee manual, the next step is to recruit, interview, and select the employee. Many new businesses jump directly to this step, which is normally a mistake. When you start interviewing potential employees, for instance, they'll often ask about your benefits package, vacation time, and in some cases even topics such as maternity leave. This is where thinking through the job and putting together an employee manual before you start interviewing pays off. If you're talking to a qualified and attractive job candidate, you don't want to come across as unprepared (or make up your policies on the fly). You want to have answers to these types of questions.

## Recruitment

The number one rule of thumb in recruiting employees is to cast a wide net, and to not rush the process. Develop a standard application form to make it easy to compare applicants. You should be looking for the best fit between a candidate's qualifications, skills and personality, and your job description and the culture of your business. There are several different

**Table 12.2.  A Sample of Employee Recruiting Options**

| | |
|---|---|
| Professional Network | Let your professional network know you're recruiting, and place a link on your Web site for applicants to retrieve and submit applications. |
| LinkedIn and other Social Networking Sites | Contact your LinkedIn contacts and use your other social networking sites to ask your network if they know anyone who might fit the profile of what you're hiring for. You can also actively search for candidates among LinkedIn members by searching on keywords for people with the required qualifications listed in their LinkedIn profiles. |
| Internet Job Boards | Job boards, such as Simply Hired, CareerBuilder.com and Monster.com, remain useful vehicles to post jobs. |
| Job Fairs | Job fairs are recruiting events that bring together employers and job-seekers in one location. They're generally sponsored by colleges or universities, professional associations, or community organizations. |
| Professional Associations | Most professional associations have some sort of job referral service, publish a newsletter listing available positions, or maintain a resume bank. |
| Classified Ads | Classified ads in newspapers and online sites remain a useful option. |
| Help Wanted Sign | A help wanted sign is appropriate if you have a retail footprint and at least a portion of the people that see the sign might be viable candidates. For example, if you're starting a retail store, your best customers may also be qualified job candidates. |

ways to get the word out about your job opening. A sample of the choices you have is provided in Table 12.2.

If you receive a large number of applicants, you'll have to find ways to reduce the applicant pool to a manageable number to interview for the job. Look for the best fit between the job you're advertising and the candidate. While this advice may seem self-evident, there are many people who apply for multiple jobs and may not be a good fit for your job, even though their cover letter and resume looks good. Also, look for people who are progressing in their career, rather than people who continually make lateral moves.

### Interviewing

Many businesses narrow their applicant pool to a dozen or so, and interview those candidates initially by phone. A phone interview can help you identify whether the candidate's qualifications, experience, workplace

**Table 12.3. Steps in a Typical Job Interview**

| | |
|---|---|
| 1. | Contact the person you want to interview and set the place and time for the interview. |
| 2. | Welcome the candidate to the meeting, and establish rapport through small talk. Explain to the candidate approximately how long the interview will take, and what you plan to achieve. |
| 3. | Ask a list of predetermined questions that you'll ask of all candidates. The questions should pertain primarily to the candidate's job qualifications and to the job. |
| 4. | Shift to situational questions, based on the particular job and your business's circumstances. For example, if you're running a fitness center, and you're hiring someone to work at the front desk, ask the job candidate what he or she would say if a member of the center said, "I'm just not convinced the center is a good value for me. I pay $85 a month and only come in once or twice a week. I'm thinking about dropping my membership." |
| 5. | Ask a handful of difficult questions (which are usually very stressful for the candidate) like, "I need to tell you that I'm interviewing five candidates for the position. Now that we've had a chance to talk, and you know more about the job, tell me why you think I should hire you opposed to one of the other four candidates?" A similarly tough question would be to ask the candidate to share a situation in a previous job where they handled a particularly difficult situation well. |
| 6. | Wrap up the interview by asking the candidate if he or she has any questions for you. If generally a red flag if the candidate doesn't have any questions. |
| 7. | Conclude the interview by providing the candidate a timeline for when you'll be making a decision. Hand the candidate a business card and thank him or her for their interest. |

preferences, and salary (or hourly wage) expectations are consistent with your position and business. The process of setting up the interview can tell you a lot about a job candidate. You'll need to correspond with the candidate (usually by e-mail) about the time of the interview and the context. This will allow you to see how the candidate handles himself or herself via e-mail and on the phone. It's a good preview for how the candidate will handle himself or herself with your customers or clients.

You'll typically invite a smaller number of candidates for personal interviews. You can interview candidates at your place of business, or at a public place such as Starbucks or Panera Bread restaurant. The way the interview process typically pans out is shown in Table 12.3.

There are a handful of questions you cannot ask in an interview, as a result of federal law. The general rule is that questions must be job-related.

Examples of questions that are illegal, along with how to get at the same information legally, are as follows:

- Illegal: "Are you a U.S. citizen? Legal: "Are you authorized to work in the U.S.?
- Illegal: "How old are you?" Legal: "Are you over the age of 18?"
- Illegal: "Are you married? How many children do you have? Who do you live with?" Legal: "Can you relocate if necessary? Can you work overtime if required?"
- Illegal: "What clubs or social organizations do you belong to?" Legal: "Do you belong to any professional organizations or trade groups that you consider relevant to your ability to perform this job?"
- Illegal: "How tall are you? How much do you weigh?" Legal: These questions are only proper if they are job related. For example, if you have to be over 5 ft. 9 inches tall to safely operate a piece of equipment that will be part of your job, then the question is job related.

You can ask applicants questions that may seem iffy if they're job related. For example, if the interview is for a job that will require driving, you can ask the applicant about his or her driving record. If the job involves handling money or spending time in your customer's homes, you can ask the applicant whether he or she has ever been convicted of a crime and the details of the conviction.

You can also conduct skills tests as part of the interview process. For example, if one of the primary tasks associated with a job is to enter information into Excel spreadsheets, you can set up a scenario and ask each candidate to enter a certain amount of information into Excel spreadsheets in a certain amount of time, and compare the results. Just make sure the candidates are aware that the skills test will be administered and they know the purpose of it.

### Selection

Selection is making the final decision, and offering the job to the top candidate. Prior to making the final decision, you should check references.

This is an essential step that is sometimes skipped, but is usually worth the time and effort. You should only make an offer if you've identified a candidate that meets the requirements of the job and you're excited about. It is better to restart the process than settle for someone who's only partially qualified or you're only mildly enthused about.

Making the offer is fun. You should do it in person or by phone, and follow up the offer in writing to avoid misunderstandings. You may make the offer contingent on a background check and drug screening, depending on the laws in your state governing these requests. You may also require that the employee sign a nondisclosure agreement as part of the terms of employment (see Chapter 2, Legal Requirements Part 2), which binds the employee to keep your business's trade secrets secret. You should allow the candidate to give his or her current employer proper notice, and provide additional time to relocate if necessary. If the candidate tries to negotiate salary or benefits, negotiate in good faith but be mindful of your budget.

Extend to the candidates you didn't hire the courtesy of letting them know the job was filled, and thank them for their interest. If you spent a considerable amount of time with one or more of the candidates that you didn't hire, you might want to call them to give them the decision and thank them for their time and effort. If you offered to cover travel expenses for the candidate who you interviewed but didn't hire make sure to reimburse the candidates promptly.

## Step 5: Complying With Regulations Pertaining to Having Employees

There are a potpourri of laws and regulations that you must comply with once you start hiring employees. These laws and regulations fall under the general category of "compliance." There is no single place where all the rules and regulations are listed. It's strictly incumbent upon you to become familiar with the rules and regulations and to govern yourself accordingly. You can hire an accountant or placement firm to help you comply, but many new businesses do not have the financial resources to pursue that route. The following are the most visible rules and regulations.

First, when you hire an employee, you must get their social security number and have them complete IRS forms W-4 and I-9. You're also required by law to report information about new employees to the appropriate agency in your state within 20 days of the employee's date of hire.

Second, the Federal Occupational Safety and Health Administration (OSHA) mandates specific health and safety standards employees must provide for the protection of employees. Many states have similar standards. The information you need is provided in OSHA's Small Business Handbook at http://www.osha.gov/Publications/smallbusiness /small-business.html. If you're unsure about how to comply with a specific standard, OSHA offers a free consultation service, including sending an inspector to your place of business.

One thing OSHA requires is the use of specific signs, depending on the nature of your business. Be particularly attentive to that part of the Small Business Handbook. Signs that warn employees and others of specific hazards are color-coded and come in distinct shapes and sizes. For example, a warning triangle, which is yellow with a black border, denotes a hazard is present such as "High Voltage." Mandatory warning signs are blue and white and they notify you that precautions must be taken in certain areas, such as "Hard Hat Required" or "Protective Eyewear Required."

Third, as mentioned in Step 1, employers must pay nonexempt (or hourly) employees no less than the federal minimum wage for each hour worked and time and one-half for work beyond 40 hours per week. There are specific exceptions. The minimum wage at the time of writing this chapter (June 2012) is $7.25 per hour. There is a special minimum wage for people under 20 years old for 90 days from the date of their employment.

Fourth, there are a number of federal laws that employers must follow when hiring employees. In a nutshell, these laws prohibit discrimination in employment decisions based on race, color, religion, sex, age, ethic/national origin, disability, or veteran status. Also, many states and cities have laws that prohibit employment discrimination based on marital status, sexual orientation, and a variety of other characteristics.

Fifth, on termination of employment, some workers and their families have the right to continue participating in your health insurance plan (if you have one) for a limited period of time. This is referred to as COBRA and is explained in Chapter 3, Getting Up and Running.

Sixth, there are posters, beyond those required by OSHA, that are required to be posted in the workplace. The U.S. Department of Labor provides an online tool to help you discern the specific posters your business is required to post: http://www.dol.gov/elaws/posters.htm.

This list is not exhaustive. You should check the Department of Labor's Web site before hiring your first employee to check current laws and regulations. A Department of Labor site designed specifically to help new businesses discern the rules and regulations they need to comply with is available at http://www.dol.gov/compliance/audience/smallbus.htm.

## Step 6: Independent Contractor Versus Employee

Anyone who works for your business is either an employee or an independent contractor. In general, an employee is someone who works for you, at your place of business, with your tools and equipment, and according to your leadership, rules, and direction. An independent contractor, in contrast, is someone who is in business for themselves, work on their own time with their own tools and equipment, and perform services for a number of different clients.

Whether you consider someone an employee or an independent contractor is an important call. It makes a difference for tax purposes. As described in Step 1, employers pay a portion of their employees' Social Security (FICA) and Medicare taxes, provide workers' compensation insurance (if they have three or more employees), and pay Federal Unemployment Tax (FUTA). They do not pay any taxes or provide workers' compensation insurance for independent contractors.

As a result of this difference, the IRS looks carefully at whether you're calling the people who work for you employees or independent contractors. It's obviously cheaper for you to call them independent contractors. You have to be careful, however, to make the right call because the IRS can levy severe penalties if workers are misclassified. There can also be penalties at the state level. This isn't to say you shouldn't use independent contractors. You should just make sure you can justify the classification.

For tax purposes, you report the income of an employee on IRS Form W-2 and the income of an independent contractor on IRS Form 1099.

One technique used by many small businesspeople is that before they hire someone full-time, they try them out as an independent contractor to see how they work out. This is sound advice, as long as the job they're given fully complies with independent contractor status. For example, if you're thinking about hiring someone as a full-time graphic designer, there is nothing wrong with first hiring the person as an independent contractor (i.e., freelancer) to complete a single project for a fixed fee. That way you get a good sense of the person's work ethic, their demeanor, and the quality of their work before you commit to full-time employment.

## Step 7: Hiring Your Spouse, Children, or Other Family Members

Many new businesses employ the founder's spouse, children, or other family members. There is nothing wrong with this, as long as a few guidelines and rules are followed.

First, you should approach hiring family members in the same manner that you would hire any employee. Their job should be budgeted for, their qualifications should fit the job description, and they should only be hired if they can legitimately do the job. You should also keep track of their time carefully (particularly if they are an hourly employee), and they should be paid just like any other employee.

If you hire one or more of your children, make sure that you don't violate federal or state child labor laws. These laws prevent hiring children younger than 18 years for hazardous jobs and establish rules for allowable hours and mandatory breaks for different age ranges. Details pertaining to child labor laws are available at the Department of Labor's Web site at http://www.dol.gov/whd/regs/compliance/childlabor101.pdf. You should also check with your state labor authorities. Some state have rules that go beyond the federal rules.

Tax laws get a little tricky when you employ a spouse or child in your business. You should check with a tax accountant to inform you about the latest laws and regulations in this area.

# APPENDIX
# First 100 Days Plan

## Postlaunch (Days 31–100)

### *Part 12: Hiring Your First Employee*

|  | Requirement | Check when done | Result (fill in below) |
|---|---|---|---|
| Step 1 | Establish a budget for position | ☐ | Identify the first employee you plan to hire (title of the position, not the name of a person). Establish a budget for the position. The budget must include base salary or hourly wage, additional employer-related costs, and benefits. Determine the total annual cost of employing the employee. |
| Step 2 | Write a job description | ☐ | Write a job description for the position identified in Step 1. |
| Step 3 | Draft an employee manual | ☐ | Write the Table of Contents for the Employee Manual you would create. |
| Step 4 | Recruitment, interviewing, and selection | ☐ | Describe the process you would use to recruit, interview, and select the employee identified in Step 1. |

*(Continued)*

## Part 12: Hiring Your First Employee (Continued)

| | Requirement | Check when done | Result (fill in below) |
|---|---|---|---|
| Step 5 | Complying with regulations pertaining to having employees | ☐ | Identify the regulations you would need to comply with regarding the employee identified in Step 1. |
| Step 6 | Independent contractors versus employees | ☐ | Describe instances in which you might use independent contractors instead of employees. Be specific. Justify the independent contractor status for the job or jobs you have in mind. |
| Step 7 | Hiring your spouse, children, or other family members | ☐ | Identify how you would handle this issue if applicable. |

# CHAPTER 13

# Day-to-Day Challenges of Operating a Business

## Introduction

This chapter focuses on day-to-day challenges of operating a business. The challenges covered are those that you'll most likely encounter in the first 100 days of a business. There are many additional challenges, such as building a staff, developing long-range plans, and growing the business, that will come as your business matures. The challenges highlighted are day-to-day challenges that you'll encounter right away and will be forced to deal with.

The following are the steps in The First 100 Days Plan covered in this chapter:

| Step 1 | Dealing with Distractions and Interruptions |
|--------|---------------------------------------------|
| Step 2 | Juggling Multiple Roles |
| Step 3 | Staying on Top of Government Regulations and Compliance Issues |
| Step 4 | Succeeding Financially |
| Step 5 | Achieving Work–Life Balance |
| Appendix | First 100 Days Plan: Day-to-Day Challenges of Operating a Business |

## Step 1: Dealing with Interruptions and Distractions

As a business owner, your days will be filled with interruptions and distractions. As a result, on most days, it will be hard to get everything done that you planned to get accomplished. Don't fight it. Dealing with interruptions and distractions is a reality of running a business. There are techniques that can be utilized, however, to make sure interruptions and distraction don't overwhelm you or derail you from important work.

Those techniques include minimizing distractions and establishing start-of-the-day and end-of-the day routines.

### Minimizing Distractions

The first step in dealing with interruptions and distractions is to minimize them. Table 13.1 contains a list of the ways in which people are distracted, and common remedies for avoiding or minimizing the distraction.

*Table 13.1. Ways to Minimize Distractions*

| Potential distraction | Remedy |
|---|---|
| Interruptions from employees, friends, family, and others | There is an old saying that "you train people how to treat you." This is true of your daily work schedule. If you set-aside certain times of the day when you don't want to be interrupted, and you're polite but strict about it, people will figure it out and be less likely to bother you during those times. |
| E-mail notifications | Many people program their smartphone so they get an audible alert when a new e-mail message comes in. Resist the temptation to do this. It's hard to resist checking to see who has e-mailed, even if you're trying to focus on an important task. |
| Dealing with nonbusiness related e-mail during the business day | Restrict your business e-mail to business-related issues. Handle your personal e-mail on a separate account, and check that account after hours. If you get a Facebook notification on your business e-mail with fresh photos of your new niece or nephew, it's just too hard to resist stopping what you're doing to look at the photos during the business day. |
| Constant flow of phone calls, text messages, incoming e-mail | Batch your responses rather than deal with them in real time. If you're working on an important project, let the phone go to voice mail. Set predetermined times during the day to answer phone calls, text messages, and e-mail. |
| Spending time trying to find something | Disorganization is one of the biggest robbers of time and attention. This is why it's important to have an organized office, an effective filing system, and an effective way to archive important e-mail. |
| Fielding inquires | If you have employees, route inquires that you don't have to personally handle to the appropriate employee. In terms of e-mail, craft and archive responses to predictable inquiries and questions. For example, if someone sends you an e-mail that says, "Tell me about the strengths of your product compared to your competitors," you shouldn't have to spend 20 min crafting an e-mail response. It's predictable question. Prepare a response, archive it, and send it out when needed. Update the response periodically to reflect any changes that are applicable. |

An exception to these remedies is if responding to e-mail and phone calls is time sensitive. For example, if you have a business where your customers ask for price quotes, and it's important that you get back to them quickly, you may need to respond to phone calls and e-mail messages in real time, unless you can delegate the task to a qualified employee. If you can't and still need uninterrupted time, you may need to schedule it before and after normal work hours.

### Establish Start-of-the-Day and End-of-the-Day Routines

One of the biggest hazards of interruptions and distractions is that they impede your ability to focus on important tasks. We've all sat down to work on something that's critically important, only to be pulled away to deal with something that's more urgent. One technique to help ensure that important tasks get done is to bookend your day with established routines at the start and end of each day. For example, say you own a printing company and your employees work from 8:30 am to 5:00 pm each day. You generally work from 7:00 am to 6:00 pm. Table 13.2 depicts what your start-of-the-day and end-of-the-day routines might look like.

*Table 13.2. Start-of-the-Day and End-of-the-Day Routines for the Owner of a Printing Business*

| Start-of-the-day routine | |
|---|---|
| 7:00 to 7:15 am | Check and respond to e-mail |
| 7:15 to 7:30 am | Review and proofread jobs that will be completed that day |
| 7:30 to 8:30 am | Work on high-priority tasks |
| 8:30 to 8:40 am | Greet employees and make sure the business is adequately staffed for the day |
| 8:40 to 9:00 am | Help get jobs started on production floor |
| **End-of-the-day routine** | |
| 4:00 to 4:15 pm | Check and respond to e-mail and phone messages. |
| 4:15 to 4:30 pm | Walk production floor to assess whether all went well during the day. |
| 4:30 to 5:00 pm | Wrap up the day by attending to any paperwork or issues that didn't get handled during the day. |
| 5:00 to 6:00 pm | Continue working on high-priority tasks. |

Note two specific things these routines accomplish. First, both the start-of-the-day and the end-of-the-day routines set aside time to work on high-priority tasks. The times are scheduled before and after employees are present and your production line is running. You'll find that it's hard to block off uninterrupted time during the middle of the day. There is just too much going on. The beginning of the day and end of the day are more controllable, so that's your opportunity to get uninterrupted time. Second, the routines establish fixed times to prevent errors and enhance quality. The start-of-the-day routine includes a 15-minute block to double-check the jobs that will be run that day (to both check for errors and to add last-minute enhancements), and the end-of-the-day routine provides a 15-minute block to walk the production floor to make sure everything is okay.

To illustrate how hard it is to schedule uninterrupted time during the middle of the day, consider the following scenario, versions of which play out in businesses each and every day. Say the printing service described here is your business. It's Friday afternoon, and you have 2:00 to 4:00 pm blocked out to work on end-of-the-month financial reports. They need to be done by Monday morning. Three months ago you secured a $50,000 line of credit at your bank, and the loan agreement requires you to submit financial statements at the end of each month. You were late last month and don't want to be late again. At 2:30 pm, just when you're making good progress, your secretary knocks on the door and says there is a call you have to take. The call is from a wedding planner. Your business printed programs for a wedding that will take place at 11:00 am tomorrow morning in a community 60 miles away. The wedding planner, who is upset, said she just noticed that the bride's first name is misspelled on the program. The bride's first name is Anne, spelled A-N-N-E. The program reads Ann, A-N-N. The wedding planner tells you that the rehearsal is in three hours, and there is no way she is going to let the bride see the program with her name misspelled. It has to be redone. You politely ask the wedding planner to wait on hold, and quickly track down the file. You check the order form and feel your heart sink. The name on the order is Anne, spelled A-N-N-E. Someone set up the proof wrong and the mistake wasn't caught. You pause in the hallway to think. There is no one available to do the job. If you start right away you can rerun the job, hit the road, and get the corrected programs to the wedding planner before the rehearsal. You pick up the phone and tell the wedding planner your plan. You think to yourself, "Now I'll have to come in over the weekend to work on the financial report, or tackle it Monday morning and hope I'm not interrupted again. I absolutely have to get the report to the bank on Monday."

This is exactly the type of scenario that business owners encounter all the time. They block out time to work on an important task, and something comes up that demands their immediate attention. The important task is then set aside. An alternative is to establish start-of-the-day and end-of-the-day routines, like those shown in Table 13.2, where time is set aside to work on important tasks when you're least likely to be interrupted. In the scenario described, if you had followed the suggested routines, you probably would have worked on the financial reports that morning during the 7:30–8:30 time slot set aside to work on high-priority tasks. In addition, if you had a practice of reviewing and proofreading all orders the morning they are run (as specified in Table 13.2), you may have caught the mistake on the wedding announcement before it was printed. An added advantage of focusing on critical tasks early in the day is that it's the time of the day where you're the most rested and alert.

The activities that comprise start-of-the-day and end-of-the-day routines will vary by business. If you're running a retail store, for example, your start-of-the-day routine may be more focused on getting the business up and running for the day. For example, if you were the manager of Pine Tree Coffee, the fictitious coffee shop described in Chapter 8, Operations, your start-of-the-day routine might involve unlocking the doors, deactivating the security alarm, adjusting the thermostat, opening the blinds, turning music on, brewing coffee to create a "coffee house" aroma, placing cash in the cash register, and so on. It might also include activities similar to those shown in Table 13.2.

## Step 2: Juggling Multiple Roles

If your business is like most start-ups, you're starting small and will be doing most of the work early on yourself. This will require you to take on all the tasks described in this book, along with additional tasks that are specific to your business. It's a lot. In fact, the need to juggle multiple roles is one of the reasons a high percentage of new businesses fail. Even if your business is simple you still must produce a product or service, sell it, develop a marketing program, manage the business's finances, maintain a Web site, pay taxes, create and maintain a professional image, make sure business licenses and permits are kept current, and the list goes on. All of this must be accomplished in a hurry-up environment. Once launched, a business can't stop while its owner gets up to speed on marketing or operations. The owner must get up to speed on these tasks quickly while at the same time juggling other responsibilities or the business will falter.

The best way to confront this challenge is a two-step approach. The first step is to discern the roles you're capable of performing. If you're a typical start-up this must be a long list, because most start-ups are resource constrained and the founder-manager must wear multiple hats. Don't underestimate yourself. There are many tasks, like managing a business's books, which look foreboding but can be handled by most people. For example, as explained in Chapter 4, Bookkeeping and Financial Management, if you use QuickBooks or another popular bookkeeping package, there are multiple written and video tutorials available to help users get up to speed quickly. The second step is to get help in areas that you feel you can't get up to speed on quickly or you feel you won't have time to accomplish. Don't be bashful—every business owner needs help in one or more areas. In some cases this will mean that you'll have to hire an employee or service to provide you the help you need. For example, if you don't feel like you have the expertise or the time to manage your own books, there are independent bookkeepers, bookkeeping services, and accountants available in most communities that you can hire who will do it for you. There is also free help available. Table 13.3 contains a list of ways that business owners gain access to skills and expertise without spending money.

*Table 13.3.  Ways Business Owners Can Gain Access to Skills and Expertise Without Spending Money*

| Technique | Explanation | Web site address |
|---|---|---|
| Bartering Arrangements | Some new businesses establish bartering arrangements with other business. For example, Chapter 2 contains an example of a consulting company that exchanged consulting services with a Web design firm to get their Web site built. | NA |
| Board of Advisors | Many businesses set up informal boards of advisors, who provide advice on a voluntary basis to help the business get up and running. The board may include an attorney, a CPA, and a human resource management specialist, for example, who meet with the founder of the firm periodically to lend assistance and advice. | NA |
| SCORE and Similar Business Assistance Organizations | SCORE is a nonprofit association dedicated to helping small businesses get off the ground. There are SCORE chapters in many locations across the U.S. SCORE will match a business owner with a SCORE volunteer who has expertise in the area the business owner is seeking, such as accounting, marketing, or management. Many local chambers of commerce and economic development commissions offer similar services. | www.score.org |
| SBDC | The Small Business Development Commission, which is a branch of the SBA, has offices in many communities that provide free consulting services to small businesses. | www.sbdc.gov |
| Joining Support Groups | There are support groups that target specific types of businesses. An example is the National Association for Women Business Owners. | www.nawbo.org |
| Participating in Online Forums | There are a growing number of online forums that provide business owners the opportunity to pose questions that other business owners answer. An example is the Startup Nation Community Forum, which sponsors forums covering multiple start-up topics. | http://www.startupnation.com/business-networking |

# Step 3: Staying on Top of Government
# Regulations and Compliance Issues

One thing that will surprise you as a business owner is the amount of time you'll spend on compliance-related issues. Compliance means adhering to government rules and regulations. It's generally the least satisfying part of running a business, but it's vital to get right to avoid penalties and civil lawsuits. You also can't plead ignorance. For example, if you're required to carry workers' compensation insurance for your employees, and the rules governing workers' compensation insurance change for your state, it's up to you to be aware of the changes and to make the necessary adjustments. The same applies for regulations enforced by the Department of Labor, the IRS, the Equal Employment Opportunity Commission, The Department of Health and Human Services, the EPA and other federal, state, and local government agencies.

The bottom line in regard to compliance is that regardless of how small your business is, you have to have a compliance strategy. You must know (a) what regulations you are subject to, (b) what you need to do to say in compliance, and (c) how you'll monitor changes.

There are several ways to discern the regulations you are subject to and what you need to do to stay in compliance. First, when you obtain your initial business licenses and permits, be sure to note the requirements for maintaining them. You should develop a system to alert you to when licenses and permits needs to be renewed, and should also periodically check the respective agencies' Web sites to see if changes are being introduced. Second, if you hire work done in an area that requires compliance with government regulations, then generally part of the value that your provider provides is to keep you current with regulations. For example, if you hire Paychex to process your payroll, they'll figure the tax withholding that are applicable for each of your employees and make adjustments when rates change. Third, as indicated throughout this book, a good source of information for the regulations that apply to your business is to speak with business owners that have businesses similar to the one you're starting. Finally, apply common sense. If your production process results in the need to dispose of hazardous material, then it is very likely that EPA rules will apply. Similarly, if you're initiating a job search for the first time, call your state's Department of Labor and ask if they publish a guidebook or support a Web site that focuses on compliance issues. The state of Iowa, for example, maintains an "Employer Awareness Guide," which provides a comprehensive directory of compliance issues for hiring employees in Iowa (http://regassist.iowa.gov/employer_aware/index.html). The 12 covered are as follows:

1. Required Work Place Postings
2. Workers' Compensation Insurance
3. Unemployment Insurance
4. Misclassification
5. Contractor Registration
6. Minimum Wage
7. Youth Employment
8. Occupational Health and Safety Administration (OSHA)
9. Tax Registration
10. I-9 Form
11. New Hire—Child Support
12. Equal Employment Opportunity (EEO)/Affirmative Action (AA)

It's clear that anyone hiring employees in Iowa would benefit from visiting this site.

## Step 4: Succeeding Financially

A business must make money to be sustainable. While this statement may seem self-evident, you'd be surprised by how many business owners don't have a firm grasp on whether their business is making or losing money. Don't fall into this group. There are three financial metrics that you should be on top of if not on a daily basis, than a weekly or monthly basis depending on how tight your finances are. The tighter your finances, the closer attention you should pay to each of these metrics. The metrics are profitability, liquidity (cash flow), and overall financial stability.

### Profitability

Profitability is the ability to earn a profit. Most bookkeeping packages, such as QuickBooks, will track your income and expenses and tell you whether you're generating a profit. You should also know the profitability of your individual product lines. For example, if you're a garage door company and you sell manual and automatic doors, QuickBooks will help you discern whether you're making more money on the manual or automatic doors. You do this by creating classes for each product line. When you enter income and expenses, you then assign them to a specific class (i.e., manual or automatic doors).

You should also know whether your profits are leading or lagging industry averages. Normally, businesses collect this information through informal conversations with industry peers or by joining industry trade groups, which typically collects information about average profitability for businesses in the industry.

It's important to track your profitability for several reasons. First, and most obvious, it tells you whether you're succeeding or failing as a business, and whether immediate corrective action is needed. Second, if you track profitability by product line, it helps in your decision making. For example, if your manual garage doors sales are losing $5,000 per month and your automatic garage doors sales are making $10,000 a month, you could potentially increase the profitability of your business by $5,000 a month by shutting down your manual garage door sales. These types of decisions are never no-brainers. You may want to maintain a limited selection of manual garage doors to preserve your status as a complete provider of garage door solutions, but may reduce your inventory and actually increase your prices to cut losses

Finally, if your profits are trailing industry averages, you should find out why. It may be that you're not operating as efficiently as peer businesses, or you may not be utilizing cost-effective marketing techniques. To the extent possible, analyzing your profitability relative to peers will help you make these types of discernments and take corrective action.

### Liquidity (Cash Flow)

Liquidity is a business's ability to pay its bills and meet its short-term financial obligations, as discussed in Chapter 11, Managing a Business's Money. As indicated in Chapter 11, a business must carefully manage its cash to make sure it has enough money in the bank to meet its payroll and cover its bills and other obligations.

Again, bookkeeping programs such as QuickBooks can be extremely helpful. QuickBooks not only maintains for you a running account of your cash balance, your accounts receivable, and your accounts payable, but also will allow you to do "what if" planning if your accounts receivable payments don't come in when they're due or sales are lower than expected. QuickBooks is flexible enough to track and analyze these numbers for any period of time. For example, many businesses pay their employees on the 15th and the last day of each month. A business owner could develop forecasts (based on projected sales, projected expenses, projected receipt of accounts receivable, and projected accumulation of accounts payable) to predict its cash balance on the 15th and the 30th of each month. QuickBooks could then track actual versus projected results on a daily basis leading up to the payroll dates, to provide the owner information about whether enough cash will be available to make payroll.

Some businesses deal with potential cash flow shortfalls by maintaining a cash reserve or by establishing a line of credit at a bank. Businesses are forced to scramble when these options aren't available. For example, if the owner of the printing business mentioned earlier in the chapter concluded that the business won't have sufficient cash at the end of the month to make payroll, he might try to make up the difference by calling the companies that owe him money and offering a discount if they pay early. Another approach would be to offer current customers a discount if they place a new order and pay in advance.

### Overall Financial Stability

Along with profitability and liquidity, a business must also remain vigilant regarding its overall financial stability. For a business to be financially stable, it must not only earn a profit and remain liquid but must also keep its debt and receivables in check and grow at a measured pace. This is an aspect of business that catches many new business owners off guard. You would think that if a business got off to a good start, increased its sales, and started making money, things would get progressively more stable. In many instance, however, just the opposite happens. Consider the printing business described in this chapter. Say the owner projects that his business will double in the next year. To make this happen, he needs more people and added equipment. The new equipment and the hiring and training of the additional people will be debt financed until the increased business generates more income. Even though the business might be better off in the long run as a result of the increased business, it's easy to see the strain that's placed on the business in the short run to get there.

## Step 5: Achieving Work–Life Balance

Most people start businesses to improve their lives—whether the goal is to pursue a particular passion, have a more flexible lifestyle, or make more money. But business ownership can also be all-consuming. Think about all the tasks and responsibility described in this book—and this book only focuses on the nuts and bolts aspects of starting a business. If not handled carefully, owning a business can easily consume the majority of a person's time and attention and negatively affect a person's marriage, family life, ability to participate in volunteer activities, and physical and emotional well-being.

Fortunately, there are steps that business owners can take to strike a healthy balance between their business and their personal lives, but there is a catch. The catch is that the steps must actually be taken—they can't be just thought about or put on a to-do list. The following are three practical suggestions for starting a business and maintaining a healthy personal life. Candidly, it's been the experience of the author of this book that people who start businesses and end up with miserable personal lives don't do any of these things. Don't let this happen to you. Take these suggestions to heart and look for additional tips and advice.

### Place Boundaries on Your Business Life

Many business owners suffer because they don't place boundaries on their business life. The enviable result is working long hours because there is always something that needs to be done. The way to solve this problem is to set a routine and stick to it. For example, depending on the nature of your business, you could set your hours for 7:00 am to 6:00 pm on weekdays. If that isn't a realistic approach, you could commit to being home every evening by 6:00 pm or commit to not working on weekends and holidays.

While you'll have to find a schedule that works for you, the overarching point is to establish a routine that separates your business life from your personal life. This approach will provide you time to unwind and will allow your family to reliably schedule activities during your free time.

### Rethink the Demands of Your Personal Life

It's not just your business life that has to yield to your personal life to make work–life balance work. Your personal life also has to adjust to your business life. One way to do this is to rethink the demands of your personal life. For example, if you work from 7:00 am to 6:00 pm on weekdays, and can afford it, you might want to hire a housekeeper to clean your house once or twice a week, to relieve yourself of that chore. Sometimes little changes can make a big difference. For example, if picking up your dry cleaning is a hassle, it may be worth it to find a dry cleaning service that picks up and drops off at your home. Even if you're on a tight budget, you may find that the time you save is worth it. Other suggestions include hiring a lawn service to take care of your lawn, buying stamps online to avoid trips to the post office, and preparing meals ahead of time and freezing them to avoid cooking, or grabbing fast food on particularly hectic days. The overall idea is to offset some of the demands that your business life places on your personal life, by freeing up time and stressors in your personal life.

### Find a Way for the Business to Run When You're Not Present

A third way to find the right balance between your business and your personal life is to put in place systems and procedures that help the business run when you're not physically present. This is a step that will take more than 100 days to put in place, but you can start working on it now. One of the worse predicaments to get into, as a business owner, is to open a store, restaurant, or similar business and base so much of the success of the business on your physical presence that you feel you can't leave while the business is open. This type of setup traps a business owner into a life of long hours, week after week, with no end in sight.

A much better approach, which you should start working not right away, is to carefully document every aspect of how the business is run and then develop systems, policies, and procedures that others can follow while you aren't physically present. This concept of creating business systems was introduced in Chapter 3, Getting Up and Running. This type of approach is what allows a business to run smoothly even when the owner isn't physically present. It's also the only way a business owner can maintain a normal life, especially if the business is open 70 to 80 hours a week, which is ordinary for a retail store or restaurant.

# APPENDIX

# First 100 Days Plan

## Postlaunch (Days 1–30)

### Part 13: Day-to-Day Challenges of Launching a Business

|  | Requirement | Check when done | Result (fill in below) |
|---|---|---|---|
| Step 1 | Dealing with Distractions and Interruptions | ☐ | Identify the ways you'll minimize distractions. Assume you've decided to establish start of the day and end of the day routines. Recreate Table 13.2 for your start of the day and end of the day routines. |
| Step 2 | Juggling Multiple Roles | ☐ | Make a list of the business roles that you feel you're capable of assuming without external help. Make a list of the business roles that you believe you'll need external help. For each role, identify if you feel you'll have to pay for the help (by hiring an employee or by outsourcing it) or whether you'll be able to obtain it for free. In those cases where you feel you'll be able to obtain the help for free (such as through SCORE or the SBCD), identify the source of the free help. |

| | Requirement | Check when done | Result (fill in below) |
|---|---|---|---|
| Step 3 | Staying on Top of Government Regulations and Compliance Issues | ☐ | Describe how your business will stay on top of government regulations and compliance issues. |
| Step 4 | Succeeding Financially | ☐ | Describe how you'll monitor your business's profitability, liquidity (cash flow), and overall financial stability. Describe, in general terms, how you'll know if your business is succeeding in each of these key areas. |
| Step 5 | Achieving Work–Life Balance | ☐ | In an effort to achieve work–life balance, describe (a) the boundaries you'll place on your business life, (b) ways in which you'll rearrange your personal life to free up time, and (c) systems you'll start putting in place now to enable your business to eventually run when you're not physically present. |

# Index

## OTHER TITLES IN OUR ENTREPRENEURSHIP AND SMALL BUSINESS MANAGEMENT COLLECTION

Scott Shane, Case Western University Collection Editor

- *Growing Your Business: Making Human Resources Work for You* by Robert Baron
- *Managing Your Intellectual Property Assets* by Scott Shane
- *Internet Marketing for Entrepreneurs : Using Web 2.0 Strategies for Success* by Susan Payton
- *Business Plan Project: A Step-by-Step Guide to Writing a Business Plan* by David Sellars
- *Sales and Market Forecasting for Entrepreneurs* by Tim Berry
- *Strategic Planning: Fundamentals for Small Business* by Gary May
- *Starting Your Business* by Sanjyot Dunung
- *Growing Your Business* by Sanjyot  Dunung
- *The Small Business Controller* by Richard O. Hanson
- *International Social Entrepreneurship: Pathways to Personal and Corporate Impact* by Joseph Mark Munoz
- *Understanding the Family Business* by Keanon J. Alderson

---

# Announcing the Business Expert Press Digital Library

*Concise E-books Business Students Need for Classroom and Research*

This book can also be purchased in an e-book collection by your library as
- a one-time purchase,
- that is owned forever,
- allows for simultaneous readers,
- has no restrictions on printing, and
- can be downloaded as PDFs from within the library community.

Our digital library collections are a great solution to beat the rising cost of textbooks. e-books can be loaded into their course management systems or onto student's e-book readers.

The **Business Expert Press** digital libraries are very affordable, with no obligation to buy in future years. For more information, please visit **www.businessexpertpress.com/librarians**. To set up a trial in the United States, please contact **Adam Chesler** at *adam.chesler@businessexpertpress .com* for all other regions, contact **Nicole Lee** at *nicole.lee@igroupnet.com*.

.

CPSIA information can be obtained at www.ICGtesting.com
Printed in the USA
BVOW07s1337081213

338255BV00006B/15/P